MALONEY STADIUM MOMENTS

Dave Leone

To my GREAT friend SUE:
BEST WISHES ALWAYS!
David Leone

Copyright Notice

Dave Leone: Phillipsburg, New Jersey 08865

Dave Leone (2014-09-01). Maloney Stadium Moments. Dave Leone

Acknowledgements

Information for this book was obtained from the football website "statelinerfootball.com", the book "Phillipsburg High School Football 1905-1969" by Joe Marchetto, the Easton Express, the Express-Times, the Newark Star Ledger, the Bethlehem Globe-Times, the Allentown Morning Call, the Phillipsburg Free Press, Phillipsburg football programs, Thanksgiving Day football programs, and Phillipsburg High School yearbooks.

Phillipsburg High School

Special thanks to photographers Ralph Woodruff, Carl Baxter, Reinhold Radke, Tom Corcoran, Anthony Doran, Chuck Zovko, Athena and Adam Kita, Jim Paulus, Lors Studio, Fisk Camera Shop and Darren Leone for use of their photos. Thanks also to BSG Custom Designs for use of their Phillipsburg 100th Anniversary logo.

*Note: some photos are of unknown origin.

Also, thanks to Ed McNally for use of some programs, and to the staff at the P'burg and Easton libraries for their help with microfiche.

Special thanks to Bart Palamaro of indieauthorsupport.com for all of his assistance in getting this book published.

Dedication

Phillipsburg High School and Bellis Field at Maloney Stadium

This book is dedicated to all who have contributed to the legacy of Phillipsburg football over the past 109 years: players, coaches, fans, students, trainers, managers, cheerleaders, and band members alike. Together, Maloney Stadium and Phillipsburg football have created a remarkable history and tradition that will forever bring honor and glory to Phillipsburg High School and the community of Phillipsburg. Hopefully this tradition will continue to thrive and enhance the Phillipsburg football legacy that all P'burg fans have come to love.

CONTENTS

Mike Maloney - The Father of Phillipsburg Football

Coach Mike Maloney

Phillipsburg's first coach, Mike Maloney, guided the football program as head coach and mentor from 1905-1931. Maloney's teams posted an overall record of 106-77-17 during his tenure. His 1918 team was the first team ever to be crowned New Jersey state champion. Following his stint as head coach, Maloney assumed the duties of principal of Phillipsburg High School, and also served as athletic director. Maloney was one of the original founders of the New Jersey State Interscholastic Athletic Association, or NJSIAA, the governing body that oversees scholastic sports in the Garden State. He was one of the state's leaders in establishing age requirements for scholastic athletics in the state of New Jersey. His tireless efforts in starting, building, and guiding Phillipsburg's football program earned him the distinguished title of "Father of Phillipsburg Football." He left a legacy of hard work, commitment and dedication to the town and the school he loved. In honor of his work in establishing the football program, P'burg's football stadium was named in his honor.

Maloney Stadium

Phillipsburg football has made an indelible footprint on the New Jersey gridiron landscape for more than 100 years. During that span, the program has chalked up 650 victories, making it the winningest program in Garden State history.

In the program's infancy, starting in 1905, the team played its games at various fields around town, including North End Field, Standard Field, Ingersoll Field, and Schultz Field. Then, in 1924, the team moved to its present location on Hillcrest Blvd., where it played its games in an open field that featured bleacher-type seats accommodating a little over 1,000 fans. No fence or field house existed.

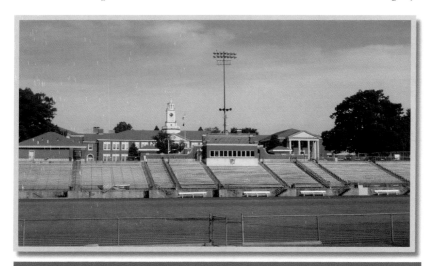

Bellis Field at Maloney Stadium, one of the most picturesque settings in all of New Jersey high school football.

Under the guidance of coach Mike Maloney, known as the "Father of Phillipsburg Football", the fortunes of the football program were upgraded when a fence, field house and permanent bleachers were installed, creating in effect what was known as Maloney Field.

The formal dedication of the historic stadium took place on October 18, 1930 when P'burg hosted Plainfield. According to P'burg football historian Joe

Marchetto, the cost to build the stadium amounted to $125,000.00. The stadium had an initial capacity of 5,316 on the home side with an additional 1,010 seats on the visiting side.

A milestone was reached in 1939 when lights were installed, allowing the team to play its first-ever night game versus Hackettstown on September 15, 1939. Since that historic contest 75 years ago, Friday night football at Maloney Field has become a ritual for thousands of Phillipsburg football fans.

In October, 1993, the field house at the east end of the stadium was named in honor of former P'burg star Jim Ringo, who was inducted into the Pro Football Hall of Fame in 1981.

The stadium then underwent a complete renovation during the 1995-1996 seasons, during which time the Stateliners played their home games at Easton's Cottingham Stadium. Upon reopening in 1997, it was rededicated as Maloney Stadium. Then, in 2007, the field was named in honor of retired legendary coach Harold Bellis, who guided the Phillipsburg program from 1954-1967. Thus, the stadium is now known as Bellis Field at Maloney Stadium.

Jim Ringo
Fieldhouse Dedication

October 15, 1993
Phillipsburg, NJ

The only meeting ever between Hackettstown and P'burg that took place on September 15, 1939 marked the first night home game that Phillipsburg ever played. P'burg wanted to open the season using a newly-installed lighting system, but the original opponent, Newark East Side, refused to play a night game, so the game with Hackettstown was quickly arranged instead. The Tigers, led by legendary coach Chot Morrison, beat P'burg 32-7 behind the play of two-time all-state FB Joe Stanowicz, who later became an All-American lineman at West Point during the Glen Davis-Doc Blanchard era The lighting system was eventually replaced by a new system in 1956.

Since its baptism in 1930, Maloney Stadium has played a prominent role in the storied history of Phillipsburg High School football. From October 18, 1930 through the 2013 season, P'burg has put together an incredible record of 332-91-15 at this beautiful venue, a winning percentage of .758. Of P'burg's 332 wins at Maloney Stadium, loyal Stateliner fans have had the honor of witnessing firsthand wins #200, #300, #500, and #600, a 21-7 win over Hillsborough in 2007.

A lifetime of thrills and memories has been created in this historic stadium with the beautiful, colonial red brick school house serving as a back drop to the contests that have captured the passion of thousands of die-hard P'burg football fans over the years. For decades, Friday nights in this football-crazy town have come to be identified by the scent of hot dogs, hot chocolate and pipe smoke in the crisp, fall air. Hopefully, the football tradition that has been created at Maloney Stadium by the hundreds of Phillipsburg athletes who have competed on the gridiron and the thousands of loyal fans who have packed the stands to root for their beloved Stateliners will continue for generations to come.

Jim Ringo Field House, named in honor of P'burg's legendary Pro Football Hall of Fame inductee

1930 Maloney Field Dedication

Logo courtesy of BSG Custom Designs.

A Century of Success

Not many schools have competed on the gridiron for 100 years or more. Phillipsburg reached that incredible milestone in 2004. To celebrate, the Stateliners kicked off their 100th year of football on September 10, 2004 when they hosted long-time rival Northampton, Pa. before a capacity crowd at Maloney Stadium. Pre-game festivities featured several members of the United States Military Academy Black Knights Parachute Team landing at midfield with the game ball, a POW-MIA flag, and a US flag that flew over Kandahar, Afghanistan on September 11, 2003. In honor of P'burg's century of excellence on the gridiron, the Stateliners wore throwback uniforms dating back to the 1930s and 1940s. To the

Stateliners wore throwback uniforms on opening night in 2004. Photo by Darren Leone.

fans' delight, a sign proclaiming Phillipsburg the "Winningest High School Program" in New Jersey

9

was unveiled and posted near the scoreboard. In celebration of the school's centennial year of football, former Stateliner football players were introduced to the crowd prior to each home game after being greeted at a reception on the lawn in front of the high school. The reception allowed former teammates to get together and talk about the good old days. The festivities represented a fitting tribute to all those who contributed to the school's historic football tradition, and brought about a great sense of pride as well as nostalgia for all of the Liners' faithful fans.

The Phillipsburg football story officially began in 1905 under coach Mike Maloney, after whom its football stadium is named. According to Phillipsburg football historian Joe Marchetto, the first team to represent the town was formed in 1889, and was comprised of "anyone in town who wanted to play." Such pickup teams existed through 1904, until the school's first official team was unveiled in 1905. Maloney, known as the "father of Phillipsburg football", was also an original founder of the NJSIAA, the body which oversees scholastic sports in New Jersey. The highlight of the school's first twenty-five years of competition came in 1918 when Phillipsburg was formally recognized by the NJSIAA as itsfirst New Jersey state champion. Maloney (106-77-17) also guided P'burg to its 100th win with a 13-0 victory over rival Easton in 1929.

A packed house was on hand on September 10, 2004 for the season opener vs. Northampton in celebration of P'burg's 100th year on the gridiron. Photo by Darren Leone.

Maloney was succeeded by Art Pursel from 1932-35, at which time Phillipsburg established itself as a state power. During his tenure, Phillipsburg won 29 straight games, and was declared state champion along with Bloomfield in 1935 after a 10-0 campaign. The program fell into mediocrity from 1936-39 until Frank Klein took over in 1940.

During Klein's eleven years as coach, Phillipsburg reestablished itself as a state powerhouse, going 84-20-9 while winning four Big 4 championships as well as a state title with Bloomfield and East Orange in 1942. Klein led P'burg to victory #200, a 19-0 win over Paterson Central in 1946. Phillipsburg also was named North Jersey co-state champions with Montclair in 1949. The 1949 team (9-0) is regarded by many long-time observers as the greatest team in garnet and grey history.

After a brief stint by Sammy Moyer, the 50's ushered in the era of Harold Bellis. The Lafayette graduate espoused a conservative philosophy, emphasizing a strong running game, defense, and sound special teams. Bellis' teams were usually small in stature, but were hard-nosed, tenacious, and well-coached. Bellis compiled a record of 86-29-10, which included a state title in 1960, and another undefeated team in 1964. Another highlight in Bellis' distinguished career came when he led P'burg to its 300th win in school history, a 42-18 romp over Allentown, Pa. in 1961. After fourteen successful years at the helm, Bellis retired following the 1967 season.

After former Phillipsburg star Mickey Frinzi led the team for five seasons, which included Big 5 co-championships in 1971 and 1972, another former standout, Bob Stem, took over in 1973 and continued the school's winning tradition. Stem's teams compiled a 56-30-4 record, which included a sectional title in 1977. During Stem's term, the Stateliners joined the East Penn League, which was comprised of all Pennsylvania teams, where they would compete through the 1994 season. In 1979, Stem guided the Stateliners to win #400, a 35-18 win over Allentown Central Catholic.

Following Stem's resignation in 1981, the Stateliners were guided by Phil Rohm from1982-86. Phillipsburg proceeded to win the East Penn League title three consecutive years in 1982, 1983, and 1984. Although they had outstanding teams, Phillipsburg was not eligible for the New Jersey state playoffs because the school was banned for competing against an all-Pennsylvania schedule.

Tom Dominic assumed the reigns from 1987-89, going a stellar 25-8 during his three years. During his term, the P'burg-Easton Thanksgiving Day game was televised live on ESPN to a national audience in 1988. Dominic resigned after the 1989 year and was succeeded by Bruce Smith, who coached from 1990-1997. His first year produced an East Penn League title in 1990, but the program languished in mediocrity except for a 9-2 record in 1994. The Liners picked up win #500 under Smith, a 39-24 victory over Emmaus, Pa. in 1993. His tenure included two years where P'burg played its home games at archrival Easton's Cottingham Stadium while Maloney Stadium underwent a complete renovation. During his stint, the school also left the East Penn League after the 1994 season, and joined the Skyland Conference in New Jersey, once again becoming eligible for state playoffs.

Phil Rohm began his second stint as head coach in 1998, and with less talent than is customary, experienced back to back losing seasons, including the worst record in school history (2-8) in 1999. Rohm quickly put the program back on track, however, tying for the league title in 2000. His encore in 2001 produced another sectional title in the North Jersey Section 2 Group 4 championship game, a 10-7 victory over 11-0, #2 ranked Montclair in a bruising defensive battle at Rutgers Stadium. Rohm's final two teams finished 9-1 in 2003, losing only in the state playoffs to eventual sectional champion Ridge, and 10-2 in 2004, losing its final two games to Easton and to Piscataway 27-26 in OT in the sectional title game, which capped off Phillipsburg's first 100 years on the gridiron.

Phillipsburg has always been known as a blue-collar, sports-oriented town. The town derives much of its image and reputation from its high school's athletic teams, especially its football program. One thing is always certain when the football season arrives: the faithful fans of this football-crazy community will turn out in droves to support their beloved Stateliners.

The first 100 years of Phillipsburg football represent a history rich in tradition. The Stateliners have produced countless championships, great players, timeless memories, a lifetime of friendships, and a reputation for toughness and excellence that has been well-documented and is well-known around the entire state. Hopefully, the next 100 years will continue that tradition and will be just as memorable as the first 100.

Maloney Stadium Moments

The following contests represent some of the most exciting
games ever played at Maloney Stadium

November 11, 1944 - P'burg 16 Bethlehem 13

P'burg head coach Frank Klein's troops entered the 1944 season coming off a 7-2 loss to Easton on Thanksgiving Day 1943, a loss which ended the Garnet and Grey's 29-game unbeaten streak.

But as was usually the case throughout the decade of the 1940's, the cupboard was brimming with talent. The P'burg starting lineup would include future NFL all-pro Bill Walsh, future all-state selections Ray Mantone, Gene Gallagher, and Mickey Frinzi, who would go on to serve as head coach and athletic director at P'burg, and diminutive halfback Dutch Seip, who would eventually climb his way into the top ten scorers of all-time.

The rivalry between P'burg and Bethlehem was intense and fiercely competitive. Two of the previous seven games played prior to 1944 had ended in ties, and three others had been decided by just seven points. Staying true to that script, the November 11, 1944 match up between the once-beaten Garnet and Grey and the unbeaten Hurricane was another close affair with the game being decided in the last two minutes.

Bethlehem got things rolling right off the bat by driving 75 yards for a touchdown following the opening kickoff. Starting at their 42, DeAngelis scampered 21 yards on second and 11 to the P'burg 38. After picking up first downs at the P'burg 24 and then the 12, Ampietro scored on an end run from the 2 to give the Hurricane the lead at 6-0. Finn's dropkick for the PAT was wide.

14

1944 action. Photos by Ralph Woodruff and Ed Williamson

P'burg responded by driving into Bethlehem territory when Mickey Frinzi ran 23 yards to the Hurricane 48. The drive stalled, however, and Frinzi punted to the Bethlehem 15.

Unable to move, Bethlehem's Ampietro attempted to punt, but the kick was blocked by Gino Conti and recovered by end Gene Gallagher in the end zone for a Garnet touchdown. Al Geist was true with the point after and P'burg led 7-6.

Bethlehem started in P'burg territory on their ensuing possession when Barth ran Bill Walsh's kickoff back 26 yards to the P'burg 49. But the Hurricane once again were unable to move the ball and punted.

The game settled into a defensive struggle through the second period with P'burg taking a 7-6 lead into the break.

Bethlehem took the lead on their second possession of the third quarter, starting at their 34. The Hurricane moved to a first down in P'burg territory, with Fritchman then bolting 48 yards up the gut to give Bethlehem the lead 12-7. Finn's dropkick was good making it 13-7.

1944 (7-1-1)

P'burg vs Northampton, Pa.	W	20 - 6
P'burg vs Lincoln (J.C.)	W	35 - 0
P'burg vs Scranton Tech, Pa.	W	51 - 0
P'burg vs New Brunswick	W	22 - 0
P'burg at Allentown, Pa.	L	12 - 0
P'burg vs Barringer	W	41 - 7
P'burg vs Asbury Park	W	27 - 6
P'burg vs Bethlehem, Pa.	**W**	**16 - 13**
P'burg vs Easton	T	0 - 0

Two possessions later, Frinzi punted to the Bethlehem 16 to start the fourth quarter. A 15-yard holding penalty on the next play set the Hurricane back to their 1. From there, Bethlehem coach John Butler decided to take an intentional safety and get a free kick from his own 20, bringing P'burg back to within 13-9.

P'burg returned the short kick back to the Bethlehem 35 where the Garnet began its winning drive with just over two minutes left in the game. On third and 3, Frinzi attempted to pass, but with no receivers open, elected to run. The fleet Frinzi swept right end, dodging several tacklers, then cut back to the left and raced untouched down the middle of the field to score and give P'burg the lead 15-13. Geist converted the point after and P'burg led 16-13.

Bethlehem had one last possession to pull out the victory and preserve the Hurricane's unbeaten season. Three attempted passes were incomplete, and on fourth down Finn was unable to get a pass off before being tackled.

The Garnet then took over possession at the Bethlehem 44 and ran the remaining time off the clock with three running plays.

1944 Phillipsburg Garnet & Grey

P"burg's defense, led by Walsh, was key to this huge victory. The Hurricane running attack, which had been successful throughout a good portion of the game, was held to zero yards rushing in the fourth quarter.

The thrilling contest played in front of 8,500 fans prompted P'burg football historian Joe Marchetto to say this about what proved to be another P'burg-Bethlehem barnburner: "This Saturday afternoon Armistice Day game was a classic and rates as one of the best football games PHS has ever participated in."

This outstanding P'burg team finished with a 0-0 tie versus archrival Easton to conclude its season with a 7-1-1 record, outscoring the opposition 212-44 on the year.

Bethlehem	6	0	7	0	13
P'burg	7	0	0	9	16

Statistics

	P'burg	Bethlehem
First downs	9	8
Yards rushing	150	154
Yards passing	13	13
Passes C-A I	2-7-0	2-6-0
Fumbles-lost	1-0	1-0
Penalties	5-45	2-30

16

October 19, 1945 - P'burg 9 Allentown 0

The P'burg-Allentown football rivalry, dormant from 1916 until it recommenced in 1930, evolved into one of the most intense rivalries P'burg ever shared with an opponent.

1945 Phillipsburg Squad

The Canaries, the only public high school in the sprawling city of Allentown, were a potent Pennsylvania power throughout the 30's, 40's and into the 50's until Louis E. Dieruff High School was opened in the 1959-1960 school year. Allentown High School then became known as William Allen High School.

Guiding the program during those golden years of Allentown football was legendary coach J. Birney Crum, who coached the Canaries from 1925-1950. From 1941-1946, Crum's powerhouse football teams accumulated a phenomenal record of 60-3-3, with 40 of those 60 wins coming by shutout. During that span, Allentown outscored the opposition by an overwhelming 1,801 to 239 margin.

It was not unusual for Allentown to come into its meeting with P'burg with an unblemished record virtually every season, and 1945 was no exception. The Canaries entered this contest 5-0, having chalked up 21 straight victories, 16 by shutout, with their last loss coming two seasons prior in 1943 when they suffered an 8-0 loss to P'burg. Having achieved national recognition, and considered one of the top programs in the eastern half of the US, Crum's Canaries had come to be known as the "overage destroyers."

Coach Frank Klein's Garnet and Grey had built a reputation for themselves as well. P'burg had enjoyed a 29-game unbeaten streak from 1941 until a 7-2 loss to Easton in the last game of 1943. P'burg followed up on that streak with a 7-1-1 mark in 1944, and came into the contest with Allentown in 1945 with a 4-0 record. For the 11,000 fans who packed Maloney Stadium for this important Big 4 contest, the anticipation couldn't have been greater.

> The 1948 game between P'burg and Allentown, Pa. featured a very unusual "three opening kickoffs." The initial kickoff had to be redone because the two bands had forgotten to play the national anthem. The second attempt was voided because the stadium lights went out while the ball was in the air. The third attempt proved to be the charm. In the end, the 16,000 fans crammed into Allentown's brand new stadium watched the Canaries beat P'burg 13-7.

Allentown threatened on its very first possession of the game. The Canary drive, aided by a 15-yard unnecessary roughness penalty against P'burg, reached the Garnet 5. At that point, P'burg's defense stiffened and forced the Canaries to turn the ball over on downs at the P'burg 3.

All-state halfback Mickey Frinzi later served as head coach and athletic director at P'burg.

Following a P'burg punt that only reached its own 16, Allentown threatened yet again. The Canaries reached the P'burg 6, but a bad snap from center was fumbled and P'burg's Al Geist recovered at the Garnet 19 to thwart another Allentown scoring opportunity.

P'burg began to take control of the line of scrimmage in the second period. The Garnet started in Allentown territory following Geist's punt return, and drove to the Allentown 5 following a Canary roughness penalty. Halfback Mickey Frinzi scored from there on an off tackle play to give P'burg the lead 6-0. Geist's point after attempt was wide.

P'burg recovered the second half kickoff at the Allentown 34 when the Canaries failed to cover the kick, but failed to capitalize on the break.

Virtually the entire third period was played in Allentown territory. Frinzi's punting was a major factor as P'burg played field position and defense, continually backing the Allentown offense up deep in its own territory.

The Garnet got another break late in the third quarter after

Frinzi punted out of bounds at the Canary 7. A fumble gave P'burg possession at the Allentown 8, but the Canary defense stiffened and forced a 19-yard field goal by Geist on fourth and 12 which gave P'burg the lead 9-0.

Allentown threatened for the third time in the game in the middle of the final period. The drive reached the P'burg 4, but on fourth down Dutch Seip picked off an errant pass, running it back to the P'burg 19 to kill another Canary threat.

1945 (8-1)

P'burg vs Northampton, Pa	W	19 - 7
P'burg vs Scranton Tech, Pa	W	26 - 0
P'burg vs Edwardsville, Pa.	W	46 - 0
P'burg at New Brunswick	W	7 - 6
P'burg vs Allentown, Pa.	**W**	**9 - 0**
P'burg vs Barringer	W	14 - 7
P'burg vs Plains, Pa.	W	48 - 6
P'burg at Bethlehem, Pa.	L	19 - 7
P'burg vs Easton	W	6 - 0

Following another P'burg punt, Allentown threatened yet again. The Canaries advanced to the P'burg 36, but captain and all-state end Gene Gallagher came up with a big interception to shut the door on the Canaries. A few plays later, time expired and the upset was in the books.

P'burg's gritty defensive performance in this game was the key to the Garnet victory. Despite being badly out gained in total yards, Frank Klein's gridders came up with clutch plays throughout the contest to score what P'burg football historian Joe Marchetto referred to as "the greatest victory ever accomplished by a PHS football team-no question about it." On the season, the stubborn P'burg defense pitched four shut outs and only allowed one team to score more than 7 points in a game.

Crum, one of the legendary coaches in Pennsylvania schoolboy history, passed away in 1981, just prior to being honored for his outstanding coaching career. Two of those honors came in 1982, when he was inducted into the Lehigh Valley Football Hall of Fame. That same year, Allentown's cavernous Allentown School District Stadium, also know as ASD Stadium, was fittingly renamed J. Birney Crum Stadium.

Allentown	0	0	0	0	0
P'burg	0	6	0	3	9

Statistics

	Allentown	P'Burg
First downs	9	4
Yards rushing	60	74
Yards passing	131	5
Passes C-A I	7-17-2	1-3-0
Punts-avg.	5-36	9-35
Fumbles-lost	1-1	3-0
Penalties-yards	60	65

The 1942 game between P'burg and Allentown, Pa., which ended in a 0-0 tie, featured an incredible thirty punts, seventeen by Allentown. The game was played in a horrible rain storm that made playing conditions treacherous. The P'burg defense held Allentown to one first down, only 30 yards rushing, and 0 completions in 6 passing attempts. The tie was the only blemish on P'burg's record as the Garnet and Grey were declared co-state champion with Bloomfield and East Orange.

October 28, 1949 - P'burg 49 McKinley Tech 35

Under head coach Frank Klein, who guided the P'burg program from 1940-1951, P'burg reestablished itself as a state power following the program's decline in the late 1930's. During the decade of the 1940's, the Garnet and Grey were twice crowned New Jersey state champion, fashioned a 29-game unbeaten streak, enjoyed three unbeaten seasons, posted four once-beaten campaigns, and put together an overall record of 72-15-8 while facing a rugged schedule comprised primarily of the best teams in eastern Pennsylvania and New Jersey.

The 1942 and 1949 teams stand out as the best among all of Klein's powerhouses, with the '49 team being considered by many long-time observers as the greatest team in school history. That squad put a punctuation mark on its remarkable unbeaten, state championship season when the Garnet and Grey upended prep powerhouse McKinley Tech 49-35 in what has been called the greatest game ever played at Maloney Stadium.

All-state halfback Russ Dilts was an elusive game breaker for P'burg's 1949 unbeaten state championship team.

The two powers had met for the first time in 1947, a game which ended in a 12-12 tie. The Washington, D.C. juggernaut entered that '47 game not only unbeaten and untied, but unscored upon. But the '49 contest, which featured an offensive explosion, took the excitement to another level. This contest was so entertaining that P'burg football historian Joe

Marchetto referred to it as a game that "must be considered one of the outstanding games in PHS football history."

P'burg scored with lightning quickness on its first two plays from scrimmage to take a quick 13-0 lead. All-state running back Russ Dilts scampered 60 yards to pay dirt on the game's first play to get the ball rolling. Following a McKinley Tech possession, Leo Sokolowski dashed 70 yards for a TD on the first play of P'burg's next possession.

McKinley Tech got on the board late in the first quarter following an interception of P'burg QB Gene Harrison. The Trainers drove 50 yards in 7 plays, with fullback Ray Fox scoring from the 2 to make it 13-7.

Dilts gave P'burg some breathing room in the second quarter when he returned a punt 38 yards to the McKinley Tech 42. From there, he bolted off tackle and sped into the end zone for his second touchdown. The PAT made it 20-7.

McKinley Tech responded with a 52-yard sustained drive, once again capped off by Fox's 2-yard run to cut it to 20-14 at the half. Little did anyone know there would be more scoring in the second half than the first.

Early in the third period, P'burg scored on a safety when Fox was sacked in his own end zone to make it 22-14 P'burg.

Just a few minutes later, the speedy Dilts scampered 27 yards around left end to the 2 to give P'burg another scoring opportunity. Dilts then plunged into the end zone for his third touchdown to make it 28-14.

McKinley Tech, a prolific passing team, then drove 64 yards to paydirt, mostly through the air. They scored when Fox hit Dick Gaskell from 24 yards out to cut it to 28-21.

Back came the Garnet and Grey. End George Wilchak recovered a fumble on the Trainer 28 to set

21

P'burg up in good scoring position. Harrison passed 15 yards to Wilchak for the score, making it 35-21 at the end of the third quarter.

P'burg stretched its lead to 42-21 after a 56-yard drive when Dilts scooted 39 yards deep into McKinley Tech territory before Sokolowsky banged it in from the 1 on the first play of the fourth quarter.

McKinley Tech tried to keep pace, once again going to the air to drive 60 yards for a touchdown. Fox hooked up with Gaskell for the second time from 9 yards out to cut it to 42-28.

P'burg finished off its scoring when the Garnet and Grey drove 46 yards, capped off by Dilts' 22-yard run to pay dirt for his fourth touchdown of the game. The conversion kick was good and it was 49-28.

McKinley Tech closed out the high-scoring affair when Fox hit Gaskell yet again, this time with a 26-yard touchdown pass, to cap off a 50-point second half outburst.

P. H. S. Squad Statistics

Name	Height	Weight	Age	Year	Position
Ron Exley, Captain	5-9	185	16	50	Tackle
Russ Dilts, Captain	5-10	165	18	50	Halfback
George Wilchak	6-1	160	17	50	End
Ed Zarbanlany	6-0	242	16	50	Tackle
Paul Weisel	6-3	182	16	50	End
Jack Gardner	5-10	168	17	50	Center
Leo Sokolowsky	5-7	147	18	50	Halfback
Ernie Minardi	5-6	160	17	50	Guard
Jack Oberly	5-10	147	18	50	Fullback
Les Erdo	5-5	140	17	50	Halfback
Selwyn Morgan	5-11	171	16	51	End
Don Riley	5-11	145	16	51	Quarterback
Ed Bottos	5-8	155	17	50	Halfback
Bill Wilson	5-8	170	16	51	Tackle
Eugene Harrison	5-8	151	17	51	Quarterback
Jim Lutz	5-9	160	17	51	Center
Jim Cyphers	5-7	145	18	51	Guard
Steve Barna	6-0	155	15	51	End
Konrad Mellert	5-10	175	16	51	Guard
Bob Eisenhauer	5-11	160	17	51	End
Dick Jarvis	5-10	170	15	52	Fullback
Joe Kutzman	5-6	166	18	51	Guard
Vine DeGeorge	5-8	165	17	51	Tackle
Ken Osborne	5-7	150	16	52	Fullback
Lloyd Griffiths	6-0	145	16	50	Quarterback
Gus Trincheria	5-8	142	16	53	Halfback
Richard Barbadora	5-8	147	16	53	End
Ron Snyder	5-11	150	15	52	Center
Don Lear	5-9	142	16	51	Halfback
Jack Lutz	5-10	169	17	52	Center
Harold Johnston	6-0	179	16	52	Tackle
Jim Mock	5-7	135	17	52	Halfback
Nick Svachak	5-9	214	16	50	Tackle
Ken Lutz	5-7	138	15	53	Quarterback
Dick Frankenfield	5-10	141	15	53	End
Earl Lippincott	5-8	140	15	51	Fullback

The game's statistics told a contrasting story to say the least. McKinley Tech chalked up 15 first downs to P'burg's 4, but the Garnet and Grey was able to use its quick-strike capability to its advantage to upend their highly regarded opponent. P'burg rushed for 385 yards while McKinley Tech's Fox, characterized by the Easton Express as "one of the greatest high school passers ever to play here", completed 17 of 31 passes for 246 yards and 3 touchdowns. The 9,000 fans who packed Maloney Stadium witnessed a game that featured some outstanding offensive talent in one of the most prolific offensive displays the area had ever seen.

1949 (9-0)

P'burg vs W. Philadelphia, Pa.	W	13-0
P'burg at Bethlehem, Pa	W	13-7
P'burg at New Brunswick	W	40-12
P'burg vs Allentown, Pa	W	25-0
P'burg vs Morristown	W	13-7
P'burg vs McKinley Tech (Washington, D.C.)	**W**	**49-35**
P'burg vs Collingswood	W	29-0
P'burg at Passaic	W	20-13
P'burg vs Easton	W	33-7

This talented P'burg team, who ended Morristown's 19-game winning streak the previous week, finished off its season by ending Collingswood's 17-game winning streak 29-0 before beating Passaic 20-13 and Easton 33-7 to finish 9-0 and capture the New Jersey state championship.

22

Phillipsburg scoring: Dilts 4; Sokolowsky 2; Wilchak 1; safety by Fox; Points after touchdown: Eisenhauer 2; Bottos 3 (place kick)

McKinley Tech scoring: Gaskell 3; Fox 2; Points after touchdown: Hudgins 5 (place kick)

McKinley Tech	7	7	7	14	35
Phillipsburg	13	7	15	14	49

Statistics

	McKinley Tech	P'burg
First downs	15	4
Yards rushing	87	385
Yards passing	246	15
Passes C-A I	17-31-1	1-4-15
Punts-avg.	3-34	4-35
Fumbles-lost	3-3	2-2
Penalties-yards	35	45

1949 action photos by Carl Baxter

November 5, 1954 - P'burg 19 Bethlehem 13

The 1954 season marked the beginning of a new and exciting chapter in Phillipsburg football history as former assistant coach Harold Bellis assumed the reigns of one of the area's premier programs. Bellis had been hired as an assistant at Coatesville, Pa. in 1940, and was named head coach at Pen Argyl, Pa. in 1941. Bellis left the head coaching job at Pen Argyl to take an assistant coaching job at P'burg under former head coach Frank Klein in 1947. His ascent to the head job at P'burg would prove to be a boon to an already successful program.

Bellis welcomed more than 100 candidates to camp, which included 16 lettermen, so things looked promising for the season. Sure enough, this veteran P'burg team came into this contest with six consecutive victories, shutting out five of its opponents while outscoring the opposition by a 137-7 count.

The Hurricane were unbeaten, but had played to three ties while putting together a 4-0-3 record. Coach Warren Harris' team entered this contest handicapped by the fact that its

P'burg abandoned the single wing formation and installed the T-formation for the first time in 1945 under coach Frank Klein. Klein moved players around to adapt to the newly-installed offense, switching junior Ray Mantone from QB to guard and replacing him with senior Al Geist, who had been the fullback. Sophomore Ed Rush, who went on to become an all-state fullback at P'burg in 1947, replaced Geist. The switch of personnel proved to be very effective, as Klein led P'burg to an 8-1 record and the Big 4 co-championship, losing only to Bethlehem 19-7 in the next to last game of the season.

star runner, Andy Moconyi, the leading rusher in the entire Lehigh Valley area, was out with an injury.

The 10,000 fans who packed Maloney Field saw P'burg get off to a great start in the ballgame. The Garnet drove 52 yards to pay dirt to get on the board with quarterback Nate Snyder sneaking it in from the one. Frank Balas converted and P'burg led 7-0.

P'burg increased its lead to 13-0 early in the second period with a 9-play, 54-yard drive. Billy Opdyke fueled the drive with runs of 13 and 10 yards to the Bethlehem 20. After a one-yard loss, Snyder hooked up with end Gene Cowell on a 21-yard touchdown pass on his only pass attempt of the entire game. Balas missed the PAT.

Bethlehem wasted little time in getting back into the ballgame, moving 77 yards in 14 plays to score only the second touchdown allowed by the P'burg defense all year. The key play in the drive was a fake punt on fourth and four from the P'burg 47 when Bauder swept right end for a big gain to the P'burg 33. He eventually scored from the 2 to get the Hurricane on the board. Paul Blatnick's conversion was good, making it 13-7 P'burg.

P'burg gave itself some breathing room by scoring again before the half, covering 67 yards in just 6 plays. George Snyder's 60-yard run to the Bethlehem 6 set P'burg up in scoring position. He scored two plays later, but Balas missed the PAT again, leaving it at 19-7 at the half.

Bethlehem got back into the game once again in the third quarter with a 6-play, 67-yard drive capped by Bauder's 33-yard run. Bauder and halfback Vince Seaman did most of the damage on the ground on traps, setting the stage for Bauder's run. The kick was wide making it 19-13.

P'burg threatened twice more in the third quarter. The first threat came as a result of a 42-yard run by Opdyke to the Bethlehem 29, but a fumble at the 25 killed the scoring opportunity.

Another opportunity to score was thwarted when P'burg turned it over on downs at the Bethlehem 34.

Back came the Hurricane, threatening to take the lead. Using a spin series out of the single wing formation, they drove to the P'burg 20, mostly on the ground. After losing yardage back to the 29, a fourth down pass good for 13 yards left them short, and P'burg took over on downs.

One last chance for the Hurricane came when they were awarded an additional play even though time had expired in the contest. But a desperation pass was unsuccessful, and the Garnet had secured the victory..

With Moconyi sidelined, the P'burg defense, led by all-state lineman Don "Rich" DeGerolamo, had survived its biggest scare of the season. P'burg blanked Newark Barringer 33-0 the following week to improve to 8-0 with six shutouts, but then suffered a devastating 7-6 defeat to an Easton team that had

All-state lineman Don "Rich" DeGerolamo was one of the leaders of P'burg's once-beaten 1954 squad.

only won two games prior to the Thanksgiving Day classic. The loss, one of the biggest upsets in the storied rivalry, deprived head coach Harold Bellis of his bid for a perfect season and possible state championship in his first season at the P'burg helm.

Bethlehem	0	7	6	0	13
P'burg	7	12	0	0	19

Statistics

	Bethlehem	P'burg
First downs	14	11
Yards rushing	183	262
Yards passing	44	21
Passes C-A I	3-7-2	1-1-0
Punts-avg.	3-28	2-20
Fumbles-lost	0-0	1-1
Penalties-yards	10	25

1954 (8-1)

P'burg vs Northampton, Pa	W	19-0
P'burg vs Wilson, Pa	W	25-7
P'burg vs New Brunswick	W	20-0
P'burg at Allentown, Pa.	W	14-0
P'burg vs Newark East Side	W	26-0
P'burg vs Roosevelt (Washington, D.C.)	W	33-0
P'burg vs Bethlehem, Pa.	**W**	**19-13**
P'burg vs Barringer	W	33-0
P'burg vs Easton	L	7-6

P. H. S. SQUAD STATISTICS

No.	Name	Class	Height	Age	Weight	Position
37	BALAS, FRANK	'56	5-11	17	220	Tackle
18	BARBADORA, DON	'55	5-7	17	160	Halfback
55	BARLETTA, JOE	'56	5-11	16	175	Guard
15	BARTOS, CHARLES	'56	5-10	16	156	Halfback
22	BETHMAN, DICK	'55	5-10	17	160	End
19	BLANCO, MANUEL	'56	5-8	17	145	Halfback
51	BRONICO, TOM	'57	5-9	15	165	Fullback
21	CHARLES, DANNY	'56	5-6	15	146	Halfback
58	CHARLES, RUSSELL	'55	5-10	17	165	End
54	COWELL, GENE	'56	5-9	17	165	End
13	CUTSLER, WALTER	'55	5-8	18	156	Halfback
12	DALRYMPLE, DICK	'55	6-0	16	170	Halfback
62	DELUCA, SAL	'55	5-7	17	185	Guard
65	DeGERALMO, DON	'55	5-11	18	180	Tackle
17	FALCINELLI, ALEX	'55	5-9	16	150	End
11	FREEMAN, JOE	'55	5-6	18	140	Halfback
66	GILL, GLENN	'56	6-1	16	184	Tackle
23	HALL, BILL	'55	5-11	17	173	Guard
61	HOUCK, WOODY	'57	5-10	15	175	Center
16	JONES, TIM	'55	5-10	16	150	End
59	JONES, TOM	'55	5-9	16	160	Center
72	KENNEDY, FRANK	'56	5-8	18	185	Guard
52	MADDOCK, JOE	'56	5-9	16	165	End
24	MARCZI, BOB	'55	5-8	17	160	Halfback
53	MONTILONE, RALPH	'55	5-10	18	165	End
25	MORGAN, ED	'55	5-8	18	170	Center
10	OPDYKE, BILL	'56	5-9	16	160	Fullback
34	PIERSON, TED	'55	6-1	18	185	Tackle
35	PIERSON, TOM	'56	6-2	17	170	Tackle
68	POCH, DICK	'57	5-10	15	165	Guard
20	ROGERS, GUS	'56	5-10	16	152	Quarterback
36	RUSH, BOB	'55	5-11	17	160	Quarterback
31	SNYDER, GEORGE	'55	5-10	18	175	Fullback
14	SNYDER, NATE	'55	5-10	17	150	Quarterback
28	STEINMETZ, FLOYD	'56	6-0	16	176	Tackle
50	STUEBER, JIM	'57	5-8	16	131	Fullback
60	TERSIGNI, JOHN	'56	5-9	16	175	Guard
26	WOOTEN, BOB	'56	5-9	16	148	Halfback

PHILLIPSBURG HIGH "STATELINERS" — 1954

1954 Phillipsburg Squad

October 16, 1960 - P'burg 14 St. Francis Prep 13

The brief rivalry between P'burg and St. Francis Prep proved to be an exciting one for Stateliner fans.

The prep school powerhouse, located in Spring Grove, Pa., was small in numbers but large in football prowess. The school was home to only 185 boys, but its reputation on the gridiron was well established.

P'burg had one other meeting with St. Francis Prep during the 1956 season. Coming into that P'burg game, the Hilltoppers had just had a 21-game winning streak snapped by Bordentown Military Academy, the New Jersey prep school champion. Despite the defeat, the Hilltoppers were still a team to be reckoned with. P'burg turned its season around when it managed to come through with what was called its best performance of the year in pulling out a 14-12 victory.

The scenario on October 16, 1960 bore some similarities to 1956. St. Francis had been hammered by BMI the week before the P'burg game by a 47-6 score, the 16th straight victory for BMI. P'burg entered the game unbeaten (6-0-1), but was coming off a 0-0 tie with underdog Bethlehem, who took the Stateliners to the limit in nearly recording a major upset. St. Francis Prep would be a test of character for coach Harold Bellis' Stateliners as the Hilltoppers, with a strong starting

In 1960, P'burg's freshmen, junior varsity, and varsity teams all finished their seasons undefeated. The P'burg freshmen finished their season 7-0. The junior varsity played to a tie in four of its first five games before finishing with a 6-0-4 record The Stateliner varsity finished with an 8-0-1 record and was named North Jersey Section 2 champion. In total, the three teams finished a combined 21-0-5 on the year, which to date is the only known season that all three teams did not lose a game in the same season.

lineup, figured to provide P'burg with possibly its toughest test of the season despite the lopsided defeat the previous week.

P'burg wasted little time in scoring following the opening kickoff when the Stateliners drove 59 yards in 14 plays to take a 7-0 lead. Two passes from quarterback Herb Bagley to fullback John Bronico helped move P'burg to the St. Francis 38. Facing fourth and 1, St. Francis was called offside on three consecutive plays to advance the ball to the 13. After Bronico bulled his way to the 7, halfback Bob Havilscek scored on an off tackle play to give P'burg the lead with 6:50 left in the opening period.

Harry Smith's conversion was good, and it was 7-0 Stateliners.

St. Francis got right back in the ballgame following a punt by Joe Mariani that rolled dead at the P'burg 6. Unable to get out of the hole, Jack Emery set up to punt out of the P'burg end zone. Emery was unable to handle Bob Stout's low snap, fumbling the ball when being tackled, with Pat Lauzon recovering for the Hilltopper touchdown. A pass for the conversion fell incomplete when Bagley jarred the ball loose from Lauzon just after he caught the ball.

St. Francis took the lead in the second quarter following another Mariani punt, this one downed at the P'burg 1. P'burg elected to punt from its end zone on third down, with Mariani fielding John Eck's punt at the P'burg 30 and returning it to the 17. On second down Mariani hooked up with Parker McCourt at the 7, then watched him scamper untouched into the P'burg end zone to give St.

Francis the lead 12-7 with 6:30 left. Mariani's PAT was good to give the Hill toppers a 13-7 lead at the break.

P'burg let a golden scoring opportunity go by the boards in the third quarter after recovering a St. Francis fumble on the Hilltopper 10. But on second down, quarterback Les Kish was picked off in the end zone to kill the threat.

31

P'burg had another chance to score after Havilscek recovered a fumble at the St. Francis 36, but the Stateliners could not cash in once again.

Yet another opportunity to score presented itself when P'burg tackle Tom Allen pounced on another St. Francis fumble at the Hilltopper 33. The Liners covered the distance in 5 plays, with the key play being Bronico's 14-yard run off tackle to the 3. Bronico scored from there to tie it up, and Smith's 13th conversion of the season gave P'burg the lead 14-13 with time still left in the third period.

Neither team threatened again until St. Francis made a move to come from behind late in the fourth quarter. The Hilltoppers drove from their 6 to their 45, but a deep pass was picked off at the 10 by P'burg defensive back Dave Dalrymple, who returned it to the 25. Two plays later, P"burg ran out the clock, surviving a major scare while maintaining its unbeaten record.

Turnovers played a major role in the win, as St. Francis fumbled 6 times, losing the ball on four occasions. Dalrymple's interception gave P'burg 5 takeaways in the ballgame.

The Stateliners would go on to edge undefeated Easton 7-6 in one of the best match ups ever in the historic Thanksgiving Day rivalry to finish the season undefeated. Smith's conversion proved to be the difference once again.

At season's end, both Bronico and Allen were named first-team all-state. To cap off the remarkable year, coach Harold Bellis' Stateliners won the Big 5 championship and were declared North Jersey Section 2 state champions.

Scoring:
1st Qtr.
P'burg…Havilscek, 7 run (Smith kick) **St. Francis**…Lauzon, fumble recovery in end zone (pass failed)
2nd Qtr.
St. Francis…McCourt, 14 pass from Mariani (Mariani kick)
3rd Qtr.
P'burg…Bronico, 3 run (Smith kick)

St. Francis Prep	6	7	0	0	13
P'burg	7	0	7	0	14

Statistics

	St. Francis Prep	P'burg
First downs	11	12
Yards rushing	135	128
Yards passing	67	27
Passes C-A I	5-9-1	5-8-1
Punts-avg.	3-31	5-32
Fumbles-lost	6-4	2-1
Penalties-yards	65	25

1960 (8-0-1)

P'burg vs Northampton, Pa	W	7-0
P'burg vs Memorial (W.N.Y)	W	12-0
P'burg vs New Brunswick	W	14-0
P'burg at William Allen, Pa.	W	14-7
P'burg at Somerville	W	20-13
P'burg vs Demarest	W	41-13
P'burg vs Bethlehem, Pa.	T	0-0
P'burg vs St Francis Prep,Pa	**W**	**14-13**
P'burg vs Easton	W	7-6

September 22, 1961 - P'burg 27 Northampton 24

Through the years, P'burg has enjoyed many rivalries with schools west of the Delaware River. Besides Easton, Bethlehem, and Allentown, another Pennsylvania program that P'burg enjoyed a long, intense rivalry with is Northampton.

The rivalry between the Stateliners and Konkete Kids dates all the way back to 1940. Prior to the 1961 season, the two teams met every year except 1949, with P'burg dominating the series, winning 17 of the 20 games played. Of all the games between the two schools, P'burg's season-opening contest with Northampton on September, 22, 1961 was without question the most exciting in the series, which thrived until the Liners joined the Skyland Conference in 1995.

Coach Harold Bellis' Stateliners were coming off an unbeaten state championship season in 1960. In the process of being named state champions, they had snapped Northampton's 17-game winning streak in the first game of the 1960 season. With coaches, players, and fans alike chomping at the bit for the start of the '61 season, the barnburner that ensued with Northampton was the perfect start to the season to the delight of the 9,500 fans in attendance.

Herb Stecker, an all-state selection in 1961, later starred at Syracuse U.

Al Erdosy's squad, operating out of the short punt formation featuring deception and slick ball handling, took an early 6-0 lead when Charlie Wogenrich set the Kids up with a 41-yard punt return. They proceeded to drive 39 yards for the opening score of the game with Frank Herzog scoring form the 6. The PAT was unsuccessful.

P'burg responded with a 6-play, 63-yard drive that was capped off with a 40-yard TD pass from quarterback Les Kish to running back John Eck, which tied it at 6-6.

Wogenrich put the Kids back on top when he dashed 51 yards to pay dirt early in the second quarter. Again the PAT was unsuccessful.

Official Program

Maloney Stadium
Friday, September 22nd, 1961
8 p.m.

PHILLIPSBURG
vs.
NORTHAMPTON

Once again, the Stateliners came back following a 30-yard punt return by Eck. They drove 38 yards with Kish scoring on a keeper from the 4. Eck's kick gave P'burg the lead 13-12 at the half.

Northampton took charge in the third quarter, driving 73 yards to take the lead again. Carl Kremus scored from 20 yards out, and the Kids led 18-13 after three quarters.

P'burg regained the lead in the fourth quarter when Dave Dalrymple sprinted 29 yards to set P'burg up deep in Northampton territory. Art Woepple scored from the 4, and Eck's kick made it 20-18 P'burg.

Wogenrich wasn't done yet, however. He scored again on a 27-yard bootleg to put Northampton back on top 24-20 late in the fourth quarter.

P'burg, showing its mettle one more time, drove for the winning score with time running out. This time Kish, who would later star at Lehigh University, hit end Dale Bodai with a 16-yard touchdown pass for the game winner that made the final score 27-24 Liners.

The winning touchdown marked the fourth time P'burg had come from behind in the game. The last minute comeback by the Stateliners negated a great performance by Wogenrich, who carried 14 times for 180 yards.

For sheer excitement, this back and forth game, which featured five lead changes, was memorable from start to finish.

Northampton	6	6	6	6	24
P'burg	6	7	0	14	27

Statistics

	Northampton	P'burg
First downs	12	15
Yards rushing	281	220
Yards passing	6	73
Passes C-A I	2-4-0	3-8-1
Punts-avg.	4-31	3-35
Fumbles-lost	1-0	1-0
Penalties-yards	10	15

1961 (7-2)

P'burg vs Northampton, Pa	**W**	**27-24**
P'burg at Memorial (W.N.Y)	W	13-6
P'burg at New Brunswick	W	28-0
P'burg vs William Allen, Pa.	W	42-18
P'burg vs Somerville	W	45-12
P'burg at East Orange	L	13-0
P'burg at Bethlehem, Pa.	W	41-0
P'burg vs Allentown Dieruff,Pa	L	19-7
P'burg vs Easton	W	7-0

1961 Phillipsburg Squad

October 9, 1964 - P'burg 0 New Brunswick 0

When P'burg and New Brunswick squared off on October 9, 1964, it marked the 21st consecutive year the two New Jersey powers had met. P'burg held a commanding 17-3-2 lead in the series, which was marked by many close, low-scoring ballgames. True to form, the 1964 showdown before 8,000 spectators would prove to be yet another game characterized by tough, stingy defense.

Both teams came into the contest with unblemished records. Coach Al Rinaldi's Zebras, known for their size and speed, had shut out Bayside (NY) 26-0 and Edison 14-0, and were looking for their first win over P'burg since 1959.

1964 P'burg all-state center/linebacker George Hummer, an all-PAC 8 pick at Arizona State, played in the North-South All-America Game and the East-West Shrine Game.

P'burg started off the season by blanking Northampton 42-0 before knocking off highly-regarded Brick Township 34-13. Coach Harold Bellis' Stateliners, coming off a 7-1-1 season in 1963, had a nice core of lettermen returning which had raised expectations for a banner season. As luck would have it, this game would probably cost this outstanding P'burg team a shot at a state championship.

New Brunswick posed the game's first real scoring threat when it started at its own 39 on its second possession. The Zebras moved to the Liner 47 before quarterback Dave Powers hit end Moe Haskins for 15 yards and a first down at the P'burg 32. Two runs gave them another first down at the P'burg 21. Powers then had a pass deflected, but halfback Don Highsmith caught the deflected ball at the P'burg 6, giving the Zebras a first and goal. They advanced to the 3, but P'burg's outstanding inside linebacker, George Hummer, came through with two huge plays, making two tackles behind the line of scrimmage to push the ball back to the 5. On fourth down, halfback Lou Haynes was stopped a yard short of the goal line by defensive backs Mickey Marino and Steve Jerolaman, and P'burg dodged a bullet.

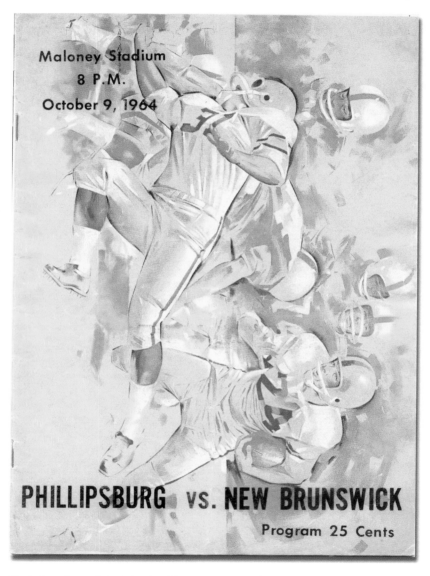

Maloney Stadium
8 P.M.
October 9, 1964

PHILLIPSBURG vs. NEW BRUNSWICK

Program 25 Cents

P'burg got it going offensively in the second period. A pass interference penalty on New Brunswick gave the Liners a first down at their 43. Quarterback Greg Seifert then hit Jerolaman with a 14-yard strike to the New Brunswick 43, and a personal foul moved it to the Zebra 28. Two plays lost two yards before Seifert hit end Don Korbobo for 8 yards to the 22. But on fourth down Seifert lost 2 yards on a rollout and New Brunswick had repelled the Stateliner drive, sending the two teams into the break locked in a scoreless tie.

The third period was uneventful until Seifert suffered an injury and was transported to Warren Hospital. Behind junior backup quarterback Bill Dukett, the Liners started a drive from their own 35. Dukett kept the drive alive twice with keepers that moved them to a first down at the New Brunswick 43. Two more Dukett keepers earned a first down at the Zebra 26. But from there the Liner march would stall. Three straight pass attempts fell incomplete before Bob Stankowski picked off an errant Dukett pass on the 23 to kill the threat.

On their ensuing possession, New Brunswick tried a quick kick on third down which was blocked and returned to the Zebra 20 by Hummer, setting the Liners up with a chance to break the ice. A clipping penalty moved the ball back to the 35. To the dismay of the packed house, the scoring opportunity went by the boards when two runs and two incomplete passes left the Liners short of a first down at the Zebra 22.

Following that threat, three consecutive possessions, two by New Brunswick, resulted in turnovers. P'burg's Skip Hall intercepted Powers at the New Brunswick 45, but three plays later Don Highsmith picked off Dukett to give the ball back to the Zebras.

1964 (8-0-1)

P'burg vs Northampton, Pa	W	42-0
P'burg vs Brick Twp	W	34-13
P'burg vs New Brunswick	**T**	**0-0**
P'burg at William Allen, Pa.	W	35-19
P'burg at Somerville	W	33-0
P'burg vs East Orange	L	27-0
P'burg vs Bethlehem, Pa.	W	33-14
P'burg at Allentown Dieruff,Pa	W	13-0
P'burg vs Easton	W	7-0

On first down, P'burg linebacker Sonny Wilson intercepted Powers yet again, giving the Liners one last chance to claim victory. A clipping penalty moved them back to their 26. Dukett hit Korbobo for 23 yards, but once again the drive stalled before time ran out in this brutal defensive battle.

In a game marked by fierce defensive play, five turnovers proved to be key in allowing New Brunswick to record its third consecutive shutout and P'burg its second in three games. The hard-hitting P'burg defense, which held the Zebras to just 129 total yards, posted six shut outs on the year.

The Stateliner defense was led by linebacker George Hummer, a first-team all-state selection who earned all-PAC 8 honors at Arizona State and was then selected in the NFL draft by the St. Louis Cardinals.

New Brunswick won the next two meetings in 1965 and 1966 before P'burg reeled off six consecutive wins from 1967-1972, the last time the two rivals ever met on the gridiron.

New Brunswick	0	0	0	0	0
P'burg	0	0	0	0	0

Statistics

	New Brunswick	P'burg
First downs	9	8
Yards rushing	79	132
Yards passing	50	43
Passes C-A I	4-9-2	3-13-3
Punts-avg.	6-29	5-3
Fumbles-lost	0	0
Penalties-yards	40	30

November 12, 1976 - Whitehall 13 P'burg 7

The first-ever meeting on the gridiron between unbeaten Whitehall and P'burg on November 12, 1976, featuring two of the leading offenses in the East Penn League, had huge ramifications.

Coach Joe Gerencser's Zephyrs (8-0, 7-0 EPL), the top-ranked team in the Express area rankings and the #2-ranked team in Pennsylvania, needed a win to clinch the conference championship and preserve their unbeaten season. P'burg, on the other hand, needed a victory to keep its hopes for a share of the league crown and a berth in the New Jersey sectional playoffs alive.

The Whitehall wishbone offense, which had scored 55 points on three occasions while outscoring the opposition 297-42, was led by senior quarterback Bob Cole (5-11, 157). Despite being at the helm of a running offense, Cole had completed 30 of 50 passes for 11 touchdowns on the season. Cole had been tabbed by Gerencser as the best quarterback in the area following a 33-0 win over Allentown Dieruff. As if to confirm his coach's boast, Cole played a pivotal role in Whitehall's 55-3 destruction of Allentown Central Catholic the week prior to the P'burg game by completing 7 of 7 passes for 175 yards and 3 touchdowns.

Steve McNamee, a 1976 first-team all-state selection, and Easton Express Player of the Year, starred at William & Mary.

Whitehall's defense had also been outstanding in its first eight contests.

40

Tough to score on, the Zephyr D, led by linebackers Bruce Rarig (6-2, 205) and Steve Panik (6-2, 205) had held every opponent to one touchdown or less, and had allowed only 3 total points in its last two ballgames.

The Stateliners (5-2) came into the ballgame on a roll, having won four straight following a slow start. The Liners, who had struggled in early season losses to Parkland 10-7 and Bethlehem Freedom 20-8, had averaged 29 points per game in their five wins. Coach Bob Stem wasn't hesitant to air things out with strong-armed senior quarterback Mike Stocker (6-1, 175), who had completed 59 of 115 passes for 753 yards and 11 touchdowns. Stocker's favorite target was senior split end Steve McNamee (5-11, 182), who had hauled in 35 balls for 441 yards and 8 touchdowns. A versatile 2-way performer who also had returned one interception and had run back two punts for touchdowns, McNamee was considered one of the best all-around players in the Lehigh Valley.

The game, played before a Maloney Stadium crowd of 8,000 on Homecoming, developed into a hard-hitting defensive battle almost from the outset. A scoreless deadlock in the middle of the second period was suddenly broken when McNamee, as heady a player as the Liners have ever had, got P'burg on the board with a 52-yard punt return for a touchdown that electrified the crowd. Watching a Zephyr punt slowly rolling almost to a stop, trailed by a host Whitehall players, McNamee suddenly scooped the ball up to the surprise of the Zephyr defenders and scampered 52 yards to pay dirt to the delight of the Stateliner faithful. Steve Searfoss converted the PAT and P'burg took a 7-0 lead into the break.

The defensive struggle continued through the third period and into the fourth quarter when the Whitehall offense, held to just 85 yards at the half and just 23 more in the third quarter, suddenly came to life.

Starting at their own 23 with just over six minutes left following a P'burg punt, Cole hooked up with split end Willie Roman to get the Zephyrs on the board. Roman hauled in Cole's pass over the middle, eluded McNamee's tackle and sprinted 77 yards for a touchdown to bring Whitehall to within a point.

Gerencser, looking for an unbeaten season, decided to bypass a kick for the tie and instead went for two. But defensive back Ed Mamrak tipped Cole's pass, leaving the Liners clinging to a 7-6 lead.

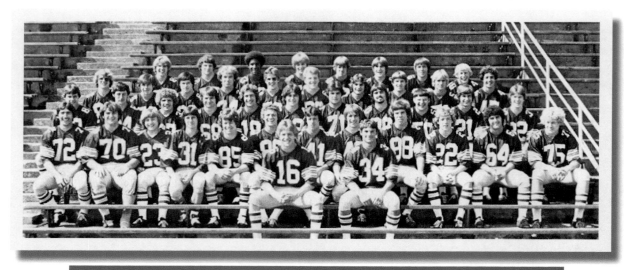

1976 Phillipsburg Squad

The Zephyrs got the ball right back following a Liner three and out. Starting at their 30, and with time running out in the game, Cole hit halfback Ed Podorsky with a 26-yard screen pass to get things going. Two completions to Roman and a 10-yard run by Podorsky moved Whitehall to the Liner 1. From there, halfback Paul Ziegenfuss dove into the end zone with just 23 seconds left to give the Zephyrs the lead and derail the Liners' upset bid. The winning drive was aided by three off side penalties against the Stateliners.

With the hard-fought win in hand, Whitehall went on to beat Emmaus and finish the season unbeaten, capturing the East Penn League championship.

The last-second loss was a heartbreaking defeat for the Liners, whose defense had shut down the potent Whitehall offense until the last six minutes of the game. Offensively, P'burg had a number of scoring opportunities, advancing to the Zephyr 24, 28, 16, 11 and 35. But 13 penalties for 92 yards doomed a great effort by the underdog Liners. Despite being knocked out of the state playoffs, the Liners regrouped to shut out archrival Easton 28-0 on Thanksgiving Day to finish their 6-3 season on a positive note.

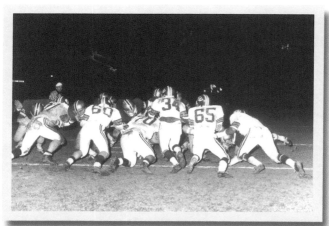

A fired-up P'burg team nearly upset unbeaten Whitehall in 1976. Photo by Tom Corcoran

Scoring:
P'burg McNamee 52 punt return (Searfoss kick)
Whitehal Roman 77 pass from Cole (pass failed)
Whitehall Ziegenfuss 1 run (Nemeth kick)

1976 (6-3)

P'burg vs Parkland, Pa	L	10-7
P'burg vs Allentown Central Catholic, Pa	W	27-6
P'burg at Freedom, Pa	L	20-8
P'burg at Bethlehem Catholic, Pa.	W	15-12
P'burg at William Allen, Pa	W	48-26
P'burg at Northampton, Pa	W	19-0
P'burg vs Liberty, Pa.	W	35-12
P'burg vs Whitehall,Pa	**L**	**13-7**
P'burg vs Easton	W	28-0

Whitehall	0	0	0	13	13
P'burg	0	7	0	0	7

Statistics

	Whitehall	P'burg
First downs	14	11
Yards rushing	123	85
Yards passing	152	54
Passes C-A I	5-13-0	5-16-1
Punts-avg.	3-35	3-38
Fumbles-lost	3	1
Penalties-yards	50	92

October 14, 1978- Allentown Dieruff 32 P'burg 23

The game between P'burg and Allentown Dieruff on October 14, 1978, pitting the league's co-champions from the previous year, was a matchup whose outcome would be pivotal in determining the East Penn League championship.

The unbeaten Stateliners (3-0), ranked 14th in the state and on a 10-game winning streak dating back to the 1977 season, were led by a dangerous passing attack featuring QB Rich Milburn, who had already thrown for 568 yards and six touchdowns, and receivers Tim Brewster and Jim Clymer, along with leading rusher Nate Johnson.

Dieruff (4-1-1) countered with an explosive rushing attack, paced by elusive running back Dave Kurisco and diminutive Manny Cole. Kurisco, just a junior, had rushed for just over 700 yards and 4 TD's coming into the ballgame. Stateliner head coach Bob Stem, who considered the tandem the best set of backs in the valley, was aware of their ability to score from anywhere on the field

In 1969, Allentown Dieruff coach Jeep Bednarik pulled his team off the Maloney Stadium field and marched them into the locker room, refusing to finish the game with Phillipsburg because he "feared a riot". The Stateliners led 7-0 when the game was abruptly halted in the middle of the 4th quarter. The actions by the Dieruff coach represent possibly the poorest display of sportsmanship ever seen at Maloney Stadium

The Liners had been dominating this series, which started in 1961, by winning four straight, and 11 of the 15 contests, with one tie. While entertaining, the highly-anticipated clash, featuring a wealth of offensive talent, would leave thousands of P'burg fans among the packed house of 8,000 spectators in the Homecoming crowd disappointed with the outcome of the high-scoring contest.

Dieruff struck first when Ray Barnard, a fleet wide receiver, raced 80 yards with a Jim Dailey punt for a touchdown with 5:16 left in the first period. A run for a 2-point conversion try was unsuccessful.

P'burg responded with a 15-play, 69-yard drive to grab the lead at the 9:23 mark of the second quarter. Key plays in the drive were a 17-yard pass from Milburn to wide receiver Tim Brewster and three pass interference calls on the Huskies. After the last infraction set the Liners up at the Dieruff one, Milburn scored on a sneak. Tom Emery's kick was true, and P'burg led 7-6.

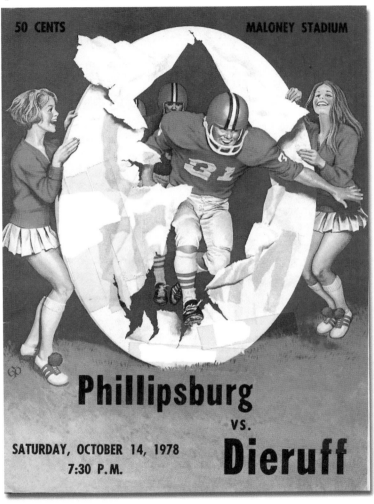

50 CENTS — MALONEY STADIUM

Phillipsburg

VS.

Dieruff

SATURDAY, OCTOBER 14, 1978
7:30 P.M.

Dieruff came right back with an 11-play drive covering 77 yards. Kurisco was a workhorse in the drive, carrying eight times and finally scoring from 23 yards out to put the Huskies up 12-7. A pass for a 2-point conversion failed.

P'burg came back quickly after Mark Williams returned the kickoff to the Liner 34. On third down, Milburn hit wide out Jim Clymer over the middle, and after breaking a tackle, he sped 66 yards down the sideline to allow the Stateliners to recapture the lead with 2:06 left in the half. Milburn then hit Mark Wilkins with a pass for a 2-point conversion to give the Liners a 15-12 lead at the break.

Dieruff capitalized on a turnover to regain the lead in the third quarter. A Milburn pass was picked off by linebacker Barry Felix and returned 11 yards to the P'burg 19. Cole gained 13 yards on first down, then Kurisco bounced outside on an off tackle play and scored from the five two plays later, giving the Huskies an 18-15 lead. Quarterback Rich Sniscak ran it in for a 2-point conversion and it was 20-15 Dieruff with 0:59 left in the third quarter.

Dieruff began to take control of the line of scrimmage in the fourth quarter. Starting at the P'burg 44 following a 14-yard punt return by Barnard, Cole swept right end for 21, then Kurisco gained 18 on another sweep for a first down at the P'burg 5. Kurisco scored from the 3 on third down, making it 26-15 and giving the Huskies some breathing room. Sniscak's run for the PAT failed.

P'burg wasn't finished yet, however. Milburn got the Liners right back in it when he led a 7-play, 69-yard drive by completing 5 of 5 pass attempts in the drive. The big play came when he hooked up with Brewster on a 22-yard strike to the Huskie 25. After moving to the Dieruff 4, Milburn hit Wilkins for the TD on second and goal to make it 26-21. Milburn's pass to Brewster for two made it 26-23 with just 3:01 to play.

The Stateliner defense was in need of a stop, but Kurisco had other ideas. On second down at the 30, he took a handoff from Sniscak and scampered 70 yards untouched down the sideline to make it 32-23 with just 2:01 left in the game.

On P'burg's ensuing possession, Barnard intercepted Milburn to put the Liners away.

Kurisco, one of the shiftiest running backs to ever play at Maloney Stadium, carried 22 times for 184 yards and four scores, proving to be too much for the P'burg defense to handle.

So impressive were the offensive fireworks that Dieruff coach Bruce Trotter called it "one of the greatest high school games you'll ever see."

Dieruff	6	6	8	12	32
P'burg	0	15	0	8	23

1978 (7-4)

P'burg vs Emmaus, Pa	W	22-13
P'burg vs Central Catholic, Pa	W	26-16
P'burg at Freedom, Pa	W	50-19
P'burg vs Dieruff, Pa.	**L**	**32-23**
P'burg at William Allen .	W	15-8
P'burg at Northampton, Pa	W	49-0
P'burg vs Liberty, Pa	W	14-13
P'burg at Whitehall, Pa.	L	33-12
P'burg at West Morris	W	36-6
P'burg vs Easton	L	14-7
P'burg vs Rahway	L	23-10

Statistics

	Dieruff	P'burg
First downs	12	11
Yards rushing	284	87
Yards passing	11	175
Passes C-A I	1-3-1	11-24-2
Punts-avg.	3-31	5-35
Fumbles lost	0	0
Penalties yards	67	35

Individual Leaders

Rushing….. Dieruff Kurisco 22-184 Cole 11-79 Gimbor 6-15
P'burg   Johnson 7-29 Williams 8-23
Honey 8-20 Milburn 8-minus 14

Passing….. Dieruff Sniscak 1-3-1 for 11
P'burg   Milburn 11-24-2 for 175

Receiving Dieruff   Reed 1-11
P'burg   Brewster 4-64 Wilkins 4-25   Clymer 3-86

Field Goals Missed…..None

D…Barnard 80 punt return (run failed)
P…Milburn 1 run (Emery kick)

D…Kurisco 23 run (pass failed)

P…Clymer 67 pass from Milburn (Wilkins pass from Milburn)

D…Kurisco 5 run (Sniscak run)

D…Kurisco 3 run (run failed)

P…Wilkins 4 pass from Milburn (Brewster pass from Milburn)

D…Kurisco 70 run (run failed)

Dave Kurisco rushed for 184 yards and 4 TDs in Dieruff's 32-23 win. Photo courtesy of Chuck Zovko.

1978 Phillipsburg Stateliners

November 5, 1982 - Bethlehem Liberty 15 P'burg 14

P'burg enjoyed a long and intense rivalry with Bethlehem, Pa. dating all the way back into the 1920's when the school was known as Bethlehem High School. The school later became known as Bethlehem Liberty in the late 1960's when Freedom High School was built. The rivalry between the two Lehigh Valley football powers continued into the 1990's until P'burg left the East Penn Conference in 1995. There were a lot of exciting games throughout the series, but the November 5, 1982 game between the two schools ranks as one of the most memorable, and painful, for Stateliner fans in the series.

P'burg entered the contest with a 6-0 record, which included shutouts of 5 of its first 6 opponents. The Liners, ranked #1 in the Easton Express area, had outscored the opposition 209-7 and were averaging 35 points per game. But it was the unheralded Hurricane that came up with the big plays to stun the Stateliners and their loyal fans with a 15-14 upset.

Liberty struck first on its second possession of the game after Danny Warren returned a P'burg punt 59 yards to the Stateliner 23. Following completions to Robert Mann and Henry Mickelson, Hurricane quarterback Steve Burns found Mickelson for a 7-yard touchdown pass to break the ice.

P'burg responded with a quick strike in the second period when Liner quarterback Chris Troxell found wide out Kenny Greene on a crossing pattern for a 76-yard touchdown. The PAT was blocked, leaving the Hurricane with a 7-6 advantage.

It remained a 1-point Hurricane lead until the fourth quarter when P'burg put together a 55-yard drive, fueled by tailbacks Tim Cummings and Bob Siemon. Those two churned out 40 yards between them before Troxell hit Greene with an 11-yard strike to the Liberty 1. Cummings scored his 11th TD from there, and Troxell hooked up with all-state end Mark Klemka on a 2-point conversion pass to give the Liners a 14-7 lead.

But the Hurricane, who came into the contest with a modest 5-4 record, weren't about to be denied.

PHILLIPSBURG vs. LIBERTY
November 5, 1982

75 Cents

They embarked on a grueling, 22-play, 80-yard drive that took nearly 9 minutes off the clock to take the lead.

Incredibly, Liberty converted four third-down plays and two fourth-down plays during the drive. Burns had completions of 11 yards to Mark Humphrey and 6, 15, and 17 yards to Robert Mann, which put the ball at the P'burg 5. Three plays later, with the ball resting on the Stateliner 2, running back Darren Smith leaped into the end zone on fourth and goal to cut the lead to 14-13 with less than two minutes remaining in the game.

That left Hurricane coach Frank Gutierrez with a big decision: should he kick the point after and forge a tie, or go for the win? For the Liberty coach, it was a no-brainer.

The Hurricane decided to roll Burns out to his right, where he hit Mike Fistner with a pass for a 2-point PAT to give Liberty the lead 15-14.

P'burg had one last chance with 1:28 left. The Liners tried to do it through the air, but 4 passes failed to gain a first down, and the Hurricane had secured the upset.

Burns came up big for Liberty, hitting 17 of 36 passes for 140 yards and one TD.

This outstanding Stateliner team, despite the crushing defeat in its last home game of the year, regrouped in a hurry, shutting out Whitehall 6-0 on the road, and routing Easton 32-0 to close out its 8-1 season with an amazing 7 shutouts in 9 games.

| Liberty | 7 | 0 | 0 | 8 | 15 |
| P'burg | 0 | 6 | 0 | 8 | 14 |

1982 (8-1)

P'burg vs Emmaus, Pa	W	28-0
P'burg vs Allentown Central Catholic, Pa	W	42-0
P'burg at Freedom, Pa	W	41-0
P'burg vs Dieruff, Pa.	W	43-0
P'burg at William Allen, Pa	W	35-7
P'burg at Northampton, Pa	W	20-0
P'burg vs Liberty, Pa.	**L**	**15-14**
P'burg at Whitehall,Pa	W	6-0
P'burg vs Easton	W	32-0

Statistics

	Liberty, Pa	P'burg
First downs	16	9
Rushes - Yards	31-75	25-57
Yards passing	140	182
Passes C-A I	17-36-2	9-20-0
Punts-avg.	4-30	4-37
Fumbles-Lost	2-0	0-0
Penalties-Yards	3-25	3-26

Individual Leaders

Rushing.....Liberty	Fistner 14-48 Smith 10-28...	
P'burg	Cummings 13-51 Siemon 9-29	
Passing.....Liberty	Burns 17-36-2 for 140	
P'burg	Troxell 9-19 for 139 Greene 1-1 for 43	
Receiving Liberty	Mann 7-81 Mickelson 4-27 Humphrey 2-18...	
P'burg	Greene 3-90 Feaster 3-56 Klemka 1-18 Souders 1-18 Cummings 1-0	
Field Goals Missed.....None		

1982 Phillipsburg Squad

Mark Klemka was a two-time all-state selection at end for P'burg.

October 5, 1984 - P'burg 14 Bethlehem Catholic 10

When Bethlehem Catholic came to Maloney Stadium to meet P'burg in an important East Penn Conference showdown on October 5, 1984, it marked the first time former Stateliner coach Bob Stem had returned to face his former team. Stem, who had resigned as P'burg coach after the 1981 season, was hoping to come away with a victory which would put the Golden Hawks in position to make a run for the conference championship.

Bethlehem Catholic (4-1) came into the contest as the favorite, having won its last 3 contests by shut out. P'burg entered the contest with a 3-1 mark, hoping to remain in contention for the league title as well. But it was the Stateliner defense that came up with the big plays to spoil Stem's homecoming.

Bethlehem Catholic scored first, in what amounted to a tough defensive struggle marked by big defensive plays, when kicker Jim Pushak nailed a 30-yard FG.

The lead was short-lived, however. P'burg put together a 14-play, 67-yard drive in the second quarter which was culminated by a 6-yard touchdown pass from quarterback Jim Horvath to tailback Tim Miers. Steve Weisel's kick made it 7-3 Liners.

Former Phillipsburg all-state and high school All-American linebacker Ned Bolcar was named Parade Magazine Defensive Player of the Year in his senior year at PHS. He later led the Fighting Irish of Notre Dame to the 1988 national title, earning All-American honors while serving as captain.

Bethlehem Catholic would take the lead before the half following a 71-yard drive. Tailback Mike

Gallagher fueled the drive with runs of 11, 11, 11 and 12 yards to put the Golden Hawks in scoring position. Tailback John McGarr ran it in from the Stateliner 2 before Pushak's kick made it 10-7 Becahi at the half.

The Hawks threatened to increase their lead in the third quarter when they put together a drive that consumed more than eight minutes of the clock. The Liner defense came up big when defensive lineman Tony Ganguzza disrupted a pitchout from quarterback Jim McCarthy to Gallagher on third and four, causing a fumble which was recovered by Liner Roger Westcott to thwart the scoring opportunity.

PHILLIPSBURG
vs.
BETHLEHEM
CATHOLIC
OCTOBER 5, 1984

DONATION
$1.00

The Liners threatened late in the fourth quarter, but Ken Godbolt picked off a Horvath pass to kill the threat at the Becahi 16. With just 3:18 remaining in the game, the Hawks were now backed up deep in their own territory clinging to the 10-7 lead. Stem, known throughout his career as a gambler, decided not to run the ball and kill some of the clock facing third down and 16 from his own 10, and also nixed the idea of taking a safety and getting a free kick from his own 20. After a time out, he decided to put the ball in the air, but with disastrous results. The pass was deflected by Stateliner defensive back Tim Hornbaker and picked off by linebacker Rob Govern, who returned it to the Bethlehem Catholic 1. Horvath snuck into the end zone from there to give the Liners the lead, and Weisel tacked on the extra point to make it 14-10 P'burg with time running down in the game.

The Stateliner D held Becahi on downs on their next possession. One last possession gave the Hawks one more shot after that, but a desperation bomb fell incomplete.

The vistory was an impressive one for the Stateliners. Their defense, led by All-American linebacker Ned Bolcar, who later starred at Notre Dame, put the clamps on the Bethlehem Catholic offense. Becahi's Gallagher managed to run for 122 yards on 25 carries, but was held to only 40 yards on 12 carries after the break.

This stingy Liner defense would allow only 84 points all season long in a 10-1 season. Including the win over Bethlehem Catholic, P'burg rattled off 9 straight wins following a 12-7 loss to Emmaus in the second week of the season and went on to capture the East Penn League championship.

Scoring
BC…..30 FG Pushak
P'burg…..Miers 6 pass from Horvath (Weisel kick)
BC…..McGarr 2 run (Pushak kick)
P'burg…..Horvath 1 run (Weisel kick)

Bethlehem Catholic, Pa	0	10	0	0	10
P'burg	0	7	0	7	14

Statistics

	Becahi, Pa	P'burg
First downs	13	11
Rushes - Yards	38-157	27-36
Yards passing	106	128
Passes C-A I	4-12-1	12-19-1
Punts-avg.	0-0	2-32.5
Fumbles-Lost	1	2
Penalties-Yards	8-73	5-38

1984 (10-1)

P'burg vs Parkland, Pa	W	21-0
P'burg at Emmaus, Pa	L	12-7
P'burg vs Central Catholic, Pa	W	35-12
P'burg at Freedom, Pa.	W	7-0
P'burg vs Bethlehem Catholic, Pa	**W**	**14-10**
P'burg at Dieruff, Pa	W	19-3
P'burg vs William Allen, Pa.	W	15-6
P'burg at Northampton,Pa	W	16-15
P'burg vs Liberty, Pa	W	16-7
P'burg vs Whitehall, Pa	W	21-7
P'burg vs Liberty, Pa.	W	16-7

Ned Bolcar was drafted in the 6th round of the NFL draft by the Seattle Seahawks.

1984 Phillipsburg Varsity

November 9, 1990 - P'burg 27 Whitehall 20

When P'burg and Whitehall met in November 1990, there was a lot riding on the outcome of the important East Penn Conference clash. The Zephyrs (9-1), ranked #2 in the Easton Express-Times area, and the 3rd-ranked Stateliners (9-1) both needed a win to keep pace with top-ranked Bethlehem Catholic (9-1), who had beaten both teams earlier in the year, for the conference title. Despite playing in the friendly confines of Maloney Stadium, the Stateliners entered the game as an underdog. Sports writer Bob Flounders, previewing the game in the Easton Express, picked the Zephyrs to win 19-7. But to the fans' delight, what was about to transpire was a P'burg comeback that had the 7,500 fans buzzing.

Things started auspiciously for Whitehall. First, Doug Bonshak got the Zephyrs off to a quick start when he returned the opening kickoff 89 yards to pay dirt. The Zephyrs then capitalized on numerous Stateliner mistakes to take a commanding 20-0 lead at the break. Dennis Lackner scored the second touchdown from the one, then Bonshak made the end zone from 2 yards out to put the Liners in a deep hole.

All-state running back Larrame Furman, who holds school records for career TDs (49) and points scored (298), scored 2 TDs in P'burg's come-from-behind 27-20 win over Whitehall.

But as often happens in games of this magnitude, momentum can swing rather quickly. On the first play of the second half, Stateliner star running back Larrame Furman ran 16 yards for only the second Stateliner first down of the game. Luckily for the Liners, the play seemed to rejuvenate the dormant P'burg offense.

Shortly thereafter, QB Tim O'Hearn lofted a pass on third and 8 to wide receiver Jim Jaroschak for a 40-yard gain to the Whitehall 23. O'Hearn then hooked up with Jaroschak in the left flat, where he broke a tackle and scored to get the Stateliners on the board. Doug Baylor's kick made it 20-7.

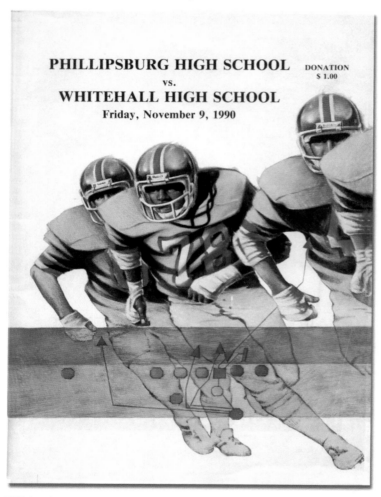

PHILLIPSBURG HIGH SCHOOL DONATION $1.00
vs.
WHITEHALL HIGH SCHOOL
Friday, November 9, 1990

On Whitehall's next series, the Liner defense came up with a huge play when defensive back Jarrod Spencer picked off an under thrown Mike Buskirk pass and returned it to the Zephyr 3. Furman then scored to pull the Liners to within 20-14 with 4:15 left in the third quarter.

P'burg forced a punt, but Jaroschak fumbled it and Whitehall recovered at the Liner 37. The Zephyrs squandered the scoring opportunity, however, when wide open receiver Chris Kocher dropped Buskirk's potential touchdown pass at the P'burg 5 on third down.

Forced to punt, P'burg's Brian Stone got off a booming 47-yard kick, but a Whitehall infraction allowed the Liners to retain possession at the Zephyr 48. From there, Furman burst over right guard, made a cut and hurdled a defender on his way to a 48-yard touchdown run that had the Stateliner faithful in a frenzy. Baylor's kick gave the Liners the lead 21-20.

With time running out and Whitehall in desperation mode, the scoring in the remarkable Liner comeback was closed out when O'Hearn picked off Buskirk's pass and returned it 30 yards for a touchdown with no time left on the clock.

Furman, a first team all-state selection, carried 22 times for 113 yards and 2 touchdowns, giving him 21 on the season, just one behind EPC record holder Dave Kurisko of Allentown Dieruff, who scored 22 in 1979. Furman's 113 yards gave him 1,285 yards on 209 carries for the year.

P'burg's second half explosion came against a Whitehall defense that was ranked #1 in the EPC. The Liner defense, on the other hand, held Bonshak, who needed just 35 yards to reach 1,000 for the season, to only 30 yards. Linebacker Doug Baylor led the Stateliner charge with 14 tackles, while the P'burg defense held the Whitehall offense to just one first down and 29 total yards of offense in the second half.

The comeback in the last home game for the Stateliner seniors, one of the biggest comebacks in P'burg football history, came against a Whitehall team that had beaten every opponent except Bethlehem Catholic by at least 21 points. The win was the key to P'burg's surge in the second half of the season that propelled them to the East Penn League championship.

Former P'burg star RB Larrame Furman is the only player ever named MVP of the Thanksgiving Day clash with archrival Easton three times. Furman garnered MVP honors on Turkey Day in three consecutive years from 1988-1990. A first-team all-state selection in 1990, Furman capped off his brilliant career at P'burg by being named the Express-Times Player of the Year. He stands as P'burg's leading scorer (298 pts.) and second leading rusher (3,515 yards) of all time. Considered by many to be the greatest running back in Stateliner history, his promising career at Louisville was cut short by a serious leg injury.

Scoring Summary

W...Bonshak 89 kickoff return (kick failed)
W...D Lackner 1 run (pass failed)
W...Bonshak 2 run (Lackner run)
P ...Jaroschak 23 pass from O'Hearn (Baylor kick)
P...Furman 3 run (Baylor kick)
P...Furman 48 run (Baylor kick)
P...O'Hearn 30 interception return (no conversion)

Whitehall, Pa	12	8	0	0	20
P'burg	0	0	14	13	27

Statistics

	Whitehall, Pa	P'burg
First downs	7	9
Rushes - Yards	32-84	35-130
Yards passing	23	73
Passes C-A I	3-11-2	5-7-0
Punts-avg.	4-32.5	4-34.5
Fumbles-Lost	1	2
Penalties-Yards	6-70	5-39

1990 (10-1)

P'burg vs Parkland, Pa	W	8-6
P'burg at Emmaus, Pa	W	18-3
P'burg vs Central Catholic, Pa	W	36-0
P'burg at Freedom, Pa.	W	27-15
P'burg vs Bethlehem Catholic, Pa	L	17-6
P'burg at Dieruff, Pa	W	27-6
P'burg at William Allen, Pa.	W	28-12
P'burg at Northampton,Pa	W	34-0
P'burg vs Liberty, Pa	W	18-7
P'burg vs Whitehall, Pa	**W**	**27-20**
P'burg vs Easton, Pa.	W	28-0

1990 Phillipsburg Squad

November 14, 2003 - Ridge 31 P'burg 27

When Ridge invaded Maloney Stadium to meet P'burg in the first round of the North 2 Group 3 playoffs in 2003, it marked the first time the two teams had ever met on the gridiron. Little did the 4,000 fans in attendance know that what was about to unfold would send shock waves reverberating throughout the Lehigh Valley and the state of New Jersey.

The consensus of opinion held that this game would be nothing more than a tune up for the unbeaten Stateliners (8-0), the section's #2 seed who came into the game ranked #2 in the Easton Express-Times and #9 in the state by the Newark Star Ledger. Ridge (8-1) entered the contest as the #7 seed, having lost to Immaculata 19-14 in the seventh week of the season. But whatever respect the Red Devils weren't accorded prior to the game was certainly earned at its conclusion.

P'burg's high-powered offense, averaging 33 points and 394 yards per game, got into high gear early, springing all-state running back Brandon Mason on touchdown runs of 62 and 88 yards to take a commanding 14-0 lead early in the second quarter. Compounding Ridge's problems, starting quarterback Tim Howarth went down with a collarbone injury in the second quarter and was replaced by backup Steve Monastero, who had not thrown a pass all year.

Brandon Mason rushed for a school-record 1,880 yards while earning 1st team all-state honors in 2003.

Monastero's transition from inexperienced backup to proven leader began to take shape in the second quarter when he connected with Joe Sutherland on a 10-yard touchdown pass. He then orchestrated another drive which was culminated with Matt Mullen's 1-yard touchdown run with just :04 left before the half to pull Ridge within 14-12.

After the teams exchanged touchdowns in the third quarter, P'burg took a 27-19 lead with 8:16 left in the game when Mason ran 29 yards for his fourth touchdown of the night.

But Monastero's heroics were still to come. First, he engineered a 65-yard drive, fueled by completions to Byron Glaspy, one for 31 yards and then another for 20 yards to the P'burg 8 on fourth and 10. The drive was capped off with an 8-yard touchdown pass to Glaspy to make it 27-25.

WELCOME TO MALONEY STADIUM   Donation $3.00

PHILLIPSBURG FOOTBALL STATELINERS

PHILLIPSBURG HIGH SCHOOL
vs.
Ridge High School
November 14, 2003
Group 3 North Jersey, Section 2 Qtr. Finals

Following a P'burg punt, Monastero directed a 76-yard drive, hitting John D'Agostini for 12 yards and Glaspy for 17. After Matt Mullen ran for 11 yards, Monastero found D'Agostini all alone in the back of the Liner end zone from 11 yards out on a blown coverage by the P'burg secondary to take a 31-27 lead. It marked the first time in the game and only the second time all season that P'burg trailed.

The Liners tried valiantly to preserve their dreams of an unbeaten season, starting on their own 30 with 1:09 left in the game. Quarterback Scott Kish (10 of 20 for 189 yards) hit Mason for 11, Steve Doran for 12, and Malcolm Dock for 14 yards before a pass interference call on Ridge put the ball on the Red Devil 14. But four plays later, a fourth down pass intended for Mason at the Ridge 5 fell incomplete, leaving the Liners and their fans stunned.

Monastero was masterful, completing 16 passes in 28 attempts for 194 yards and 3 touchdowns, with two coming in the last six minutes. His efforts negated a great performance by Mason, who rushed for 260 yards and 4 touchdowns, breaking Leonard Brice's school record of 1,638 yards rushing in a season set the previous year. Mason also tied Larrame Furman's school record of 24 touchdowns in a season set in 1990.

The devastating loss prevented P'burg, the Skyland Conference's Delaware Division champion, from achieving its first unbeaten season since 1949 when it was crowned New Jersey state champion. P'burg recovered from the loss to upend a very good Easton team 26-23 to finish the season on a winning note.

Ridge	0	12	7	12	31
P'burg	7	7	7	6	27

Statistics

	Ridge	P'burg
First downs	20	14
Rushes - Yards	34-167	43-296
Yards passing	218	189
Passes C-A I	19-32-1	10-20-0
Fumbles-Lost	3-2	2-1
Field Goals		Areola 25 yd FG
Missed		blocked

Scoring Summary

1st qtr

P'burg… Brandon Mason 62 run (Jesus Areola kick) 9:54

2nd qtr.

P'burg… Brandon Mason 88 run (Areola kick)10:23

Ridge…. Joe Sutherland 10 pass from Steve Monastero (kick blocked)

Ridge…Matt Mullen 1 run (pass failed) :04

3rd qtr.

P'burg…Brandon Mason 3 run (Areola kick) 6:53

Ridge…Monastero 5 run (Mike Buck kick) 4:38

4th qtr.

P'burg…Mason 29 run (kick failed) 8:16

Ridge…Byron Glaspy 8 pass from Monastero (pass failed) 6:12

Ridge…John D'Agostini 22 pass from Monastero (pass failed) 1:13

2003 (9-1)

P'burg at Northampton, Pa	W	39-29
P'burg vs Watchung Hills	W	42-7
P'burg at Warren Hills	W	19-7
P'burg at Bridgewater-Raritan.	W	14-6
P'burg vs Franklin	W	25-0
P'burg vs Hillsborough	W	50-3
P'burg vs Hunterdon Central.	W	31-7
P'burg at North Hunterdon	W	41-20
P'burg vs Ridge	**L**	**31-27**
P'burg vs Easton, Pa.	W	26-23

2003 Phillipsburg Varsity Squad

November 19, 2004 - P'burg 14 Elizabeth 12

The November 19, 2004 North 2 Group 4 sectional semifinal between unbeatens P'burg and Elizabeth promised to be an exciting match up. But when the dust had finally settled, the 6,000 fans in attendance had witnessed what turned out to be a classic in the first-ever meeting between the two state powers.

While Elizabeth did not have as long and storied a history as P'burg, the state's largest school had certainly had plenty of great moments on the gridiron. Formerly known as Thomas Jefferson of Elizabeth, the Union County power had won six sectional championships and had sent plenty of outstanding players on to the next level. Elizabeth's 1970 team, led by all-state guard/linebacker Richard Wood and all-state running back Gil Chapman, had gone unbeaten and been crowned NJ state champion. Wood would go on to be named first team All-American at the U. of

Tim Penyak was a Star Ledger first-team all-state selection at defensive back in 2004.

Southern California for three consecutive years and play in the NFL, while Chapman starred at Michigan.

In 2004, Coach Jeff Wiener's Minutemen entered the contest with a perfect 9-0 record and were ranked #9 in the Star Ledger, having outscored their opponents 316-69. P'burg (9-0), celebrating its 100th year on the gridiron, came in ranked #1 in the Easton Express-Times and #8 in the Star Ledger. The second-seeded Stateliners and third-seeded

Minutemen would fight it out with the winner earning the right to face the winner of the semifinal between top-seeded Piscataway (9-0), ranked #7 in the Star Ledger, and Linden.

The game started out well for the Liners when they took the opening kickoff and drove 74 yards in 14 plays to take a 7-0 lead. P'burg converted three times on fourth down in the drive, which was capped off by quarterback Scott Kish's one-yard touchdown run. Tim Burger's extra point was true.

P'burg padded its lead at the 7:44 mark of the second quarter when defensive back Steve Doran fielded a punt on the Liner 41 and dashed 59 yards along the Elizabeth sideline to pay dirt. Burger's kick made it 14-0.

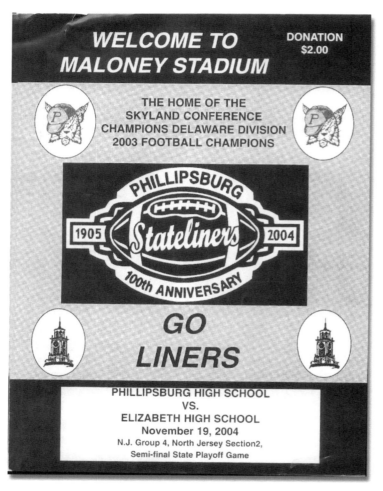

Elizabeth got back in the ballgame just before halftime when a Kish pass was tipped and then intercepted by Corey Williams, who returned it 58 yards to the P'burg 10. Elizabeth's outstanding running back Garry Warren then scored on a 2-yard run with just :27 seconds left in the half. A run for a 2-point conversion was unsuccessful leaving it at 14-6.

Elizabeth got within 14-12 with 1:42 left in the third quarter when the shifty Warren, weaving his way through the Liner defense like a water bug, scored from 11 yards out. Once again a 2-point conversion try failed.

In the fourth quarter, P'burg found itself holding on for dear life. Three times the Minutemen had the ball in Stateliner territory only to come up short each time. One apparent touchdown pass was negated when the receiver was ruled out of the back of the end zone. The last threat ended with just 1:50 left when a pass from Jerome Murphy to Williams fell incomplete.

The Liner defense, tough against the run all season long, had another outstanding effort, holding Warren, a highly-regarded junior running back drawing interest from Division 1 programs, to 77 yards on 15 carries. The Stateliners also held the potent Elizabeth offense, averaging 35 points per game, to just 12 points. The hard-fought victory advanced the Liners to the sectional final versus Piscataway, and gave them momentum heading into the annual Thanksgiving Day battle with rival Easton, who entered the contest unbeaten as well.

But the season would not end well for P'burg, who had a dismal effort versus Easton and absorbed a shocking 31-0 defeat in a battle of unbeatens. The following week, P'burg's season would come to a crashing end when the Stateliners suffered a heart-wrenching 27-26 OT loss to Piscataway in a thrilling sectional championship game at Rutgers Stadium.

Playing football at a school with the history and tradition of Phillipsburg is an honor that all players cherish for their entire lives. But for Stateliner football players in the graduating class of 2008, there was extra incentive to be proud of their careers. This group of Liners had the distinction of being part of four of the most historic events ever witnessed in P'burg's long and storied history on the gridiron. In 2004, these Liners were part of P'burg's 100th year of football. In 2005, they experienced the "perfect season", a 12-0 state sectional championship year which represents the greatest year in Stateliner history. In 2006, they participated in the 100th game between P'burg and Easton. And in 2007, they chalked up historic win #600, giving New Jersey's winningest program elite status nationwide.

| Elizabeth | 0 | 6 | 6 | 0 | 12 |
| P'burg | 7 | 7 | 0 | 0 | 14 |

Statistics

	Elizabeth	P'burg
First downs	8	13
Rushes - Yards	30-192	44-135
Yards passing	38	61
Passes C-A I	3-19-1	6-12-1
Fumbles-Lost	1-0	0-0
Punts – avg	4-27	6-28
Third down Conv	2-12	4-18
Fourth down conv	0-3	3-3
Sacks by yards	0-0	2-14
Penalties-yards	6-51	4-37

Scoring
1st qtr
P'burg............Kish 1 run (Burger kick) 1:08
2nd qtr.
P'burg...........Steve Doran 59 punt return (Burger kick) 7: 44
Elizabeth.......Gary Warren 2 run (run failed) :27
3rd qtr.
Elizabeth   Gary Warren 11 run (run failed) 1:42

Individual Statistics
Rushing ...Elizabeth Warren 15-77 Corey Williams 4-16 Antoine Thompson 3-17 Kahim Sturgis 1-4 P'burg Justin Gaymon 22-75 Scott Kish 15-45 Ian Decker 4-13
Passing...Elizabeth Pryor 3-13 for 38 P'burg Kish 6-12-1 for 61
Receiving...Elizabeth Newsom 3-38 P'burg Gaymon 2-24 Penyak 2-12 Dock 1-13 Doran 1-12

2004 (10-2)

P'burg vs Northampton, Pa	W	25-7
P'burg at Franklin	W	10-7
P'burg at Watchung Hills	W	59-16
P'burg vs Bridgewater-Raritan.	W	28-20
P'burg vs North Hunterdon	W	52-13
P'burg at Hunterdon Central	W	35-7
P'burg vs. Warren Hills	W	35-7
P'burg at Hillsborough	W	21-13
P'burg vs Woodbridge	W	34-13
P'burg vs Elizabeth	**W**	**14-12**
P'burg vs Easton, Pa.	L	31-0
P'burg vs Piscataway	L	27-26 (OT)

2004 Phillipsburg Varsity Squad

October 14, 2005 - P'burg 43 Hunterdon Central 34

The 2005 season was looked upon with optimism and great anticipation by Stateliner fans for several reasons.

P'burg returned a solid nucleus of players from their 2004 squad that lost a heartbreaking 27-26 nail biter in OT to Piscataway in the North 2 Group 4 sectional championship at Rutgers Stadium. But with a nice group of players returning, expectations were high for a successful season..

The 2005 season also welcomed former P'burg head coach Bob Stem back into the fold after a long and distinguished career at Bethlehem Catholic. Stem had gone 56-30-4, claiming a sectional title in 1977 during his first stint as P'burg head coach from 1973-1981. Stem then fashioned an impressive record of 173-56-2 while winning two PIAA titles in guiding the Golden Hawks for 19 seasons prior to returning to his alma mater.

Entering the P'burg contest, Central had put together a 4-1 record, losing to Hillsborough 22-7 while beating North Hunterdon 34-0, South Brunswick 15-0, Watchung Hills 41-7, and Bridgewater 10-7. The Red Devils needed a win over P'burg to have any shot at claiming the Delaware East Division of the Skyland Conference.

The biggest question mark facing the Liners coming into the season was the quarterback position. Over the first five games, that question had been resoundingly answered by junior Justin Viscomi, who had led the Stateliners to a 5-0 record, directing an explosive offense that had scored more than 40 points on three occasions.

The game started out with a bang for Central when P'burg lost the handle on the opening kickoff, with the Red Devils recovering. Central capitalized on the miscue by driving for the opening score, which was capped off by Matt Furstenburg's 1-yard run that gave the Devils an early 6-0 lead. AJ McNulty's kick made it 7-0 at the 6:09 mark.

P'burg responded with a game-tying drive that was finished off with Ian Decker bulling his way into the end zone from 4 yards out with :52 left in the first quarter. Tim Burger tied it up at 7-7 with a successful PAT.

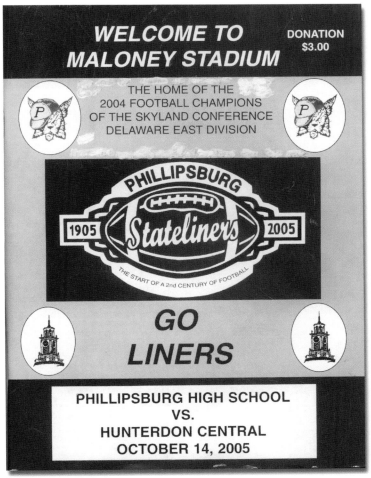

Central seized momentum with startling speed shortly thereafter, scoring 2 touchdowns in just 34 seconds. Just 24 seconds after Decker's score, Central's Chris Wynn took a wide receiver screen and sped 55 yards untouched to pay dirt to give the Devils the lead. Then QB Kyle Wachter hooked up with Justin Pennington on a 15-yard touchdown pass to give the Devils a two-touchdown lead just 6 seconds into the second period. McNulty was successful on both PATs to make it 21-7 and give Liner fans a reason to squirm in their seats.

Like all good teams, the Stateliners came roaring back as swiftly as they had fallen behind. The key play that swung momentum back into P'burg's column came on a third and 11 from the P'burg 28. Viscomi was chased out of the pocket and scampered 59 yards to the Devil 13, giving the Liners life. Tailback Art Wright scored on the very next play to make it 21-13, and Burger's kick made it 21-14 at the 10:41 mark.

P'burg's defense then forced a three and out, and the fired up Stateliners put together a 5-play, 82-yard drive to get within a point. Art Wright scored on a 21-yard run, then Ian Decker caught a 2-point conversion pass from Tyler Jones to give P'burg a 22-21 lead with 4:47 left in the half.

Central got the ball back after an exchange of possessions when Ryan Keeley picked off a Viscomi pass at the Central 47. A delay of game penalty moved them back 5 yards, then lightning struck. Wachter lofted a pass into the flat, but P'burg linebacker AJ Roberts picked it off and raced 46 yards down the sideline for a score to stun the Red Devils and send the Liner bench into a frenzy. Burger made it 29-21 P'burg to cap off a 50-point first half explosion.

Central was not finished yet, however. The Devils drove for an early TD in the third quarter with

Wachter hitting Dan Fitzsimmons from 10 yards out at the 9:03 mark. A run for a 2-point conversion was unsuccessful, leaving the score at 29-27.

P'burg came back to gain some breathing room, capping off a drive with Ian Decker's 8-yard run. Burger's kick made it 36-27 with 2:35 left in the third period.

All-state guard Eric Agnew anchored P'burg's offensive line in 2005. Photo by Athena and Adam Kita.

The drama continued in the fourth quarter. Central closed the gap to 36-33 when Furstenburg scored from 2 yards out early in the fourth. McNulty was true and it was 36-34 Liners.

Determined to close the door on the Red Devils, P'burg closed out the scoring in the fast-paced affair when Wright capped off another P'burg drive, scoring from the 6 with just 4:10 left in the game. Burger's kick capped off the scoring, allowing P'burg to escape with a hard-fought, come from behind 43-34 victory in a wild shoot out at Maloney Stadium.

The high-scoring affair was an offensive-minded fan's delight, with the two teams combining for 77 points, 36 first downs, and 761 yards of offense. Wright, an outstanding junior, led the way for P'burg with 118 yards rushing and 3 touchdowns.

This outstanding P'burg team, featuring a big, physical offensive line and talented skill position players, would go on to finish 12-0 for the first time in school history. In addition to clinching the conference championship with the win over Central, P'burg exacted revenge on Piscataway, beating the Chiefs 15-6 in a brutal defensive battle at Rutgers Stadium to capture the sectional title.

Besides their perfect season, the 2005 team set a slew of offensive records, including most points scored in a season with 422 and most yards gained from scrimmage in a season with 4,543. Individually, Viscomi, also a junior, set school records for most yards passing in a season (1,987), most TD passes in a game (5), and most TD passes in a season (17).

This talented 2005 team is without question one of the greatest teams in Phillipsburg history.

Central	14	7	6	7	34
P'burg	7	22	7	7	43

Scoring
1st qtr
HC…Matt Furstenburg 1 run (AJ McNulty kick) 6:09
P'burg…Ian Decker 4 run (Tim Burger kick) :52
HC…Chris Wynn 55 pass from Kyle Wachter (McNulty kick) :28
2nd qtr.
HC Justin Pennington 15 pass from Wachter (McNulty kick) 11:54
P'burg…Art Wright 13 run (Burger kick) 10:41
P'burg…Wright 21 run Decker pass from Tyler Jones) 4:47
P'burg…AJ Roberts 46 interception return (Burger kick) 2:19
3rd qtr.
HC…Dan Fitzsimmons 10 pass from Wachter (run failed) 9:03
P'burg…Decker 8 run (Burger kick) 2:35
4th qtr
HC…Furstenburg 2 run (McNulty kick) 11:49
P'burg…Wright 6 run (Burger kick) 4:10

Statistics

	H. C.	P'burg
First downs	17	19
Rushes - Yards	34–70	41-295
Yards passing	266	130
Passes C-A I	14-26-2	7-16-2
Fumbles-Lost	1-0	2-2
Punts – avg	5-20	2-45
Penalties-yards	2-7	6-39

Individual Statistics

Rushing…   HC: Furstenburg 17-40, Wynn 8-33, Keeley 3-2, Wachter 6-(-5);   P'burg: Wright 14-118, Decker 15-96, Viscomi 8-86 Roberts 4-25

Passing…   HC: Wachter 14-26-2 for 266;   P'burg Viscomi 7-16-2 for 130

Receiving…HC: Wynn 6-121, Pennington 4-96, Fitzsimmons 2-28, Cerulli 1-11, Aitkens 1-10;   P'burg: Woeppel 2-56, Dock 2-26, Wright 1-24, Decker 1-15, Christian 1-9

2005 (12-0)

P'burg at Northampton, Pa	W	43-21
P'burg vs Franklin	W	21-0
P'burg vs Watchung Hills	W	49-25
P'burg at Bridgewater-Raritan.	W	50-13
P'burg at North Hunterdon	W	16-6
P'burg vs Hunterdon Central	**W**	**43-34**
P'burg at. Warren Hills	W	22-10
P'burg vs Hillsborough	W	40-14
P'burg vs East Orange	W	50-20
P'burg vs Union	W	56-14
P'burg vs Easton, Pa.	W	17-0
P'burg vs Piscataway	W	15-6

P'burg-Piscataway Preview

Phillipsburg kicks off its quest for a second consecutive sectional championship and its fourth this decade when it hosts 7th-seeded Piscataway Friday night at Maloney Stadium.

Coached by Dan Higgins, Piscataway is no stranger to the Liners. Piscataway beat P'burg 27-26 in overtime at Rutgers Stadium for the North 2 Group 4 title in 2004. The Stateliners returned the favor in 2005 when they completed a 12-0 season with a 15-6 win over the Chiefs for the sectional crown.

Piscataway (4-4) is regarded in some circles as the best public high school program in the state. The Chiefs have made 17 appearances in the postseason, have reached a sectional championship game 12 times, and have won 6 titles. Four of those crowns came in the last 7 years, when they reached their sectional final 6 times. Their overall playoff record is a stellar 26-11. Entering the 2009 season, the Chiefs have accumulated a record of 107-19 over the past 15 years versus Middlesex County competition.

On an individual basis, Piscataway has produced as many Division 1A players as any school in the state in recent years. Some of those recently playing at the D 1A level include All-American cornerback Malcolm Jenkins (Ohio State), offensive tackle Anthony Davis (Rutgers), wide receiver Kyle Wilson (Boise State), and tight end J.D. Griggs (Iowa).

This year, Piscataway was selected to win the Red Division of the competitive Middlesex County Conference, and was the preseason favorite to win the sectional title. The Newark Star Ledger also ranked Piscataway #4 in the state in the preseason rankings.

This season has been an atypical one for the Chiefs, however. They have not been able to meet the lofty expectations heaped upon them, coming in at 4-4 and on a 2-game losing streak. Piscataway opened the season with a 26-14 loss to Howell Township, followed by a 14-7 loss to Sayreville. They then won four in a row, beating North Brunswick 28-15, East Brunswick 13-10, Old Bridge 44-13, and South Brunswick 28-17. The last two games resulted in losses to Woodbridge 10-3, and to Toms River North 7-0. It should be noted that Howell, Sayreville, and Toms River North have all been ranked in the state's top 20 nearly the entire season.

Piscataway has one of its youngest team in years, starting only five seniors. This is a program that is usually dominated by seniors who have been in the program for four years. With their youth, the Chiefs will be a team to be reckoned with in the very near future.

Piscataway's offense is led by quarterback Malcolm Griggs, a 6-2, 185 pound senior. Besides his offensive skills, he is a highly regarded defensive back who is being recruited by Cincinnati, Akron, Ohio State, Pitt, and Rutgers. Griggs is an athletic player who can both run and throw the ball. Griggs has a strong arm, and is adept at throwing while on the run. His best efforts this year came versus Sayreville, when he completed 8 of 13 passes for 147 yards, versus Old Bridge (9 of 12 for 184 yards and 2 TDs), and versus South Brunswick (7 of 15 for 109 yards). His favorite target is wide receiver Jawaun Wynn (6-3, 180) who has committed to play for Rutgers. Wynn's best game came versus Old Bridge, when he hauled in 6 passes for 113 yards and 2 touchdowns. Wide receiver Steve Graham, who caught 2 balls for 71 yards and a touchdown against Old Bridge, is another target.

As usual, Piscataway has another outstanding running back carrying the pigskin for them this year. Talented Anthony Tillman is an outstanding runner who can take it the distance at any time. This year, Tillman (5-9, 190) has had big games versus East Brunswick, when he rushed for 144 yards and 2 touchdowns on 26 carries, versus Old Bridge (12 carries for 108 yards and 2 TDs), and versus South Brunswick, when he picked up 151 yards and scored 3 touchdowns on 26 carries. The one thing that has plagued Piscataway this year versus a very good schedule has been a lack of consistency on offense. In their four losses, they have only scored a total of 24 points.

Defensively, this Piscataway team, although not dominant, resembles Chief teams of the past: big, fast and athletic. Their young defense has been pretty solid all year, allowing more than 17 points on only one occasion. Griggs spearheads the secondary, while linebacker Kyle Polk (6-0, 205) leads the front seven. Polk was in on more than 60 tackles last year, and had an interception return for a touchdown in their 38-0 win over Hunterdon Central in the sectional title game. He is being recruited by Akron, Pitt, Syracuse, and Boise State.

The Stateliners looked good in upending a good Bridgewater team 17-6 last week, a win that propelled the Liners to the #2 seed in the section. P'burg has been getting good efforts from a new offensive line consisting of center Joe Edinger (5-11, 248), guards Sean McNerney (5-9, 190) and Jose Mojica (5-7, 210), tackles Dylan Stair (6-2, 238) and Jeremy Stokes (5-11, 275), and tight end Johne Ringo (6-0, 195). This group has done a good job of opening holes for P'burg's running backs, and providing time for quarterback Justin Scuorzo to find his group of outstanding receivers. The Liners kept it simple last week, pounding the ball and setting up play action passes to counter the Panthers' decision to roll up their defensive backs to within four yards of the line of scrimmage. In response, Scuorzo and company burned the Panthers for 245 yards passing. The only negative last week was the Liners' inefficiency in the red zone as they failed to score from inside the Bridgewater 10 yard line on three occasions.

Defensively, P'burg's quick, young defense put the clamps on Bridgewater's running game, and held the Panthers' high-scoring offense to just six points. This week, the Stateliners will need to respect and contain Piscataway's speed at the skill positions. Keeping Griggs contained when he attempts to run out of the pocket will be a priority for this Liner defense. P'burg has done a good job of preventing big plays all year, and will need to continue that trend this week.

PREDICTION: This writer got a chance to watch Piscataway's 7-0 loss to Toms River North on television last week. The Chiefs are not a team to be taken lightly, in spite of their modest 4-4 record, which has come at the hands of a tough schedule. Their speed and athleticism make them a dangerous opponent. P'burg appears to be putting it all together at the right time. The Liners have been successful in establishing the run, and will undoubtedly try to do so again, which will open up the passing game. Barring an unexpected letdown, P'burg appears to have the edge on this Chief team, but it won't come easy. The Stateliners should be able to wear down a game Piscataway team, and move on to the sectional semifinal with a hard-earned win over a tough, well-coached opponent.

P'BURG 21 PISCATAWAY 7

November 13, 2009 - P'burg 19 Piscataway 16 (OT)

If Stateliner fans were bored with some of the Liners' easy wins over lesser opponents during the 2009 season, they certainly got their money's worth from this game.

P'burg cruised to a 16-0 lead, withstood two big plays by Piscataway that forged a 16-16 tie, then came up with two huge defensive plays before dispensing one last dose of Dana Lee to win a 19-16 OT nail-biter at Maloney Stadium to advance to the sectional semifinals.

This one had the Liner fans on the edge of their seats as they witnessed a huge momentum swing in the game that had the underdog but scrappy Chiefs on the verge of a first-round upset.

P'burg started the game off in fine fashion, putting together an opening drive that started near their 20 and took 8:43 off the clock. The Liners pounded the ball inside the Chiefs' 10, then watched running back Dana Lee run it in from the 8 to give P'burg the lead. Anthony Castro's kick made it 7-0.

The Stateliners continued to dominate the action on both sides of the ball through most of the second quarter, repeatedly shutting down Piscataway's offense and controlling the ball and the clock. But the Liners could not score again until the 2:00 mark of the second quarter, when Castro nailed a 45-yard field goal to give P'burg a 10-0 lead at the half.

The trend continued through most of the third quarter. The Stateliners then embarked on another nice drive, culminating with fullback Gerald Van DeCruz's 2-yard touchdown run that gave P'burg a 16-0 lead with just 4:12 left in the quarter. Castro's kick was wide.

Things would change drastically after that score, however. The Chiefs got good field position at their 45 on the ensuing kickoff. Just a few plays later, Piscataway's outstanding running back Anthony Tillman took a handoff while in motion after lining up on a wing, juked a host of Liner tacklers, and scampered 52 yards to pay dirt to get Piscataway on the board at the 3:20 mark. Nadir Barnwell's pass to Brandon Stout for a successful 2-point conversion brought them to within 16-8, and we had a new ballgame.

P'burg gained great field position at the Piscataway 47 following an exchange of punts, but the Liners couldn't cash in. On Justin Scuorzo's ensuing punt, freshman Kyle LaPorte fielded the ball at his 29, broke free from the grasp of a Liner tackler, eluded several others, then got outside behind a wall of blockers and raced down the Piscataway sideline for a 79-yard touchdown that left the Liners and their fans stunned. Sophomore Tevin Shaw ran the 2-point conversion try in and the game was tied 16-16.

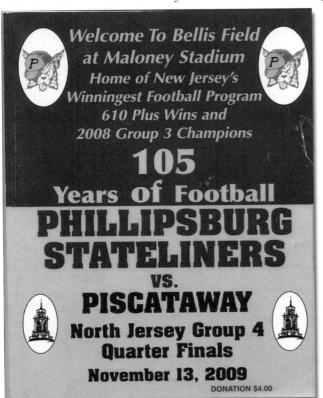

Piscataway's defense, rejuvenated after the sudden turn of events, pushed the Stateliners back inside their own 5 on their next possession. Scuorzo got off a good punt that rolled dead in Piscataway territory, where the Chiefs started on what appeared to be a game-winning drive. Piscataway moved to just outside the Liner 10 with five minutes left, but on fourth and inches, P'burg's defense got a good push up front and stuffed Barnwell for no gain on a quarterback sneak, and the Liners dodged a bullet. One more possession by each team killed the clock in regulation.

P'burg won the toss, and chose defense to start the overtime period. Starting at the P'burg 25, Piscataway was flagged for an illegal procedure penalty on first down, then Barnwell ran 10 yards to the 20. Two Tillman runs gained 3 to the 17, setting up a fourth and 2. On fourth down, Barnwell swept right end on a keeper, but VanDeCruz, a terror on defense all night with 4 tackles for loss, came up with another monster play when he ran him down from behind, and the Liners took over.

P'burg then turned to Lee, who was truly outstanding all night. He carried twice for 16 yards for a first down at the Chiefs' 9, then rushed three more times, putting the ball at the Chiefs' 3. Castro then came on and drilled a 20-yard field goal to win the game and send the Stateliner sideline into a frenzy in the most exciting game at Maloney Stadium since P'burg's 14-12 win over Elizabeth in the 2004 sectional semifinals.

Dana Lee was nothing short of spectacular, repeatedly breaking tackles while rushing for 184 yards on 26 carries. His emergence as a workhorse and as a breakaway threat was a key component in P'burg's surge during the second half of the season.

Defensively, P'burg had a terrific effort, holding Piscataway to just five first downs and 155 yards of total offense while gaining 282 themselves. P'burg did a good job of containing Piscataway's speed except for Tillman's run and LaPorte's punt return.

Piscataway gave a valiant effort in defeat, especially with Griggs on the sideline due to an ankle injury suffered earlier in the week. Just when it appeared the Chiefs were down and out, they came up with two big plays to tie it up and throw a huge scare into the Liner faithful. Tillman, bottled up for nearly three quarters, finished with 118 yards on 18 carries. Defensively, Piscataway was very quick and athletic, and got outstanding efforts from linebacker Kyle Polk and defensive end Taj Watkins, who seemed to near the ball on just about every P'burg offensive play.

This talented P'burg team closed out its 10-2 season on a high note. The Liners followed up their exciting win over Piscataway by knocking off Westfield 35-7 in their sectional semifinal at Maloney Stadium to advance to the sectional championship game. Following a 26-10 loss to Easton on Thanksgiving Day, P'burg dominated Ridge 34-7 at Keane University to capture the North Jersey Section 2 Group 4 title, the fifth sectional title in school history.

Piscataway	0	0	8	8	0	16
P'burg	7	3	6	0	3	19

Scoring
1st qtr
P'burg..........Dana Lee 8 run (Castro kick) 3:17
2nd qtr.
P'burg..........FG Castro 45   2:00
3rd qtr.
P'burg.........Gerald VanDeCruz 2 run (kick failed) 4:12
P'way.........Anthony Tillman 52 run (Brandon Stout pass from Nadir Barnwell) 3:20
4th qtr
Kyle LaPorte.. 79 punt return (Tevin Shaw run) 11:24
First OT
P'burg.......FG Castro 20

Statistics

	Piscataway	P'burg
First downs	5	19
Rushes - Yards	36-146	55-236
Yards passing	9	46
Passes C-A I	2-6-0	5-14-1
Fumbles-Lost	1-0	1-0
Punts – avg	7-25	5-38
Penalties-yards	6-39	2-29

Individual Statistics

Rushing   Piscataway: Tillman 18-118; Kyle Polk 3-22; Barnwell 10-11; Stout 4-7; Team 1-(-12).   P'burg: Dana Lee 26-184; VanDeCruz 13-40; Corman 9-31; Connell 1-2; Scuorzo 6-(-21)

Passing…Piscataway Barnwell 2-6-0 for 9; P'burg Scuorzo 5-14-1 for 46

Receiving… Piscataway: Steven Graham 2-9;   P'burg: Johne Ringo 2-28; Lee 2-9; Connell 1-9

2009 (10-2)

P'burg at Warren Hills	W	36-12
P'burg vs Franklin	W	48-6
P'burg vs Hunterdon Central	L	24-15
P'burg at Scotch Plains-Fanwood	W	40-0
P'burg vs Elizabeth	W	47-13
P'burg at Watchung Hills	W	35-7
P'burg vs Hillsborough	W	27-13
P'burg at Bridgewater-Raritan	W	17-6
P'burg vs Piscataway	**W**	**19-16 (OT)**
P'burg vs Westfield	W	35-7
P'burg vs Easton, Pa.	L	26-10
P'burg vs Ridge	W	34-7

2009 Phillipsburg Varsity Football
Photo by Lors Studio

Beyond 100 Years

In 2005, the 101st year of Phillipsburg football, expectations ran high for a successful campaign with a good nucleus of players returning from the previous season's 10-2 team. To the fans' delight, the Liners did not disappoint, as they began their second century on the gridiron with a bang. Bob Stem returned to the helm after a long distinguished career at Bethlehem Catholic, Pa., and with an abundance of talent on hand, guided P'burg to its greatest season in history with a 12-0 mark, including a 15-6 revenge victory over Piscataway for the sectional title. The Stateliners also won their 3rd straight Skyland Conference crown. Blessed with an explosive offense, stingy defense, speed, experience, and good senior leadership, this Phillipsburg team, which finished #3 in the final Star Ledger rankings, will go down in history as one of the best the school has ever produced.

The 2006 season was a near replica of 2004. The Stateliners were victorious in their first 10 games, and entered the annual Thanksgiving Day showdown with Easton @ 10-0 with a 22-game winning streak on the line. The unbeaten season and winning streak came to an end in a 21-7 loss to the Rovers, followed by a heartbreaking 14-9 loss to Elizabeth in the sectional championship game. The season was not without its highlights, however. P'burg finished at #10 in the Star Ledger final rankings. They also won their 4th consecutive Skyland Conference divisional title while running their winning streak in conference play to 29 games. Individually, quarterback Justin Viscomi became the school's all-time leader with 3,712 career passing yards and 31 TD passes. In addition, running back Art Wright broke the school record for touchdowns in a season with 26 while scoring a school record 158 points on the year, which pushed him into the #2 spot on the all-time scoring list. Five Stateliners - Viscomi, Wright, wr/db Blair Decker, fb/lb Brian Norrell, and 2-way tackle Ken Pickell received all-state mention, with Pickell being named 2nd team all-state by both the Star Ledger and Associated Press.

The 2007 season was a disappointing one, as the Stateliners completed a lackluster 5-5 season with a first round loss in state playoff action. P'burg did chalk up its state-leading 600th win in school history, however, with a 21-7 win over Hillsborough. But the Liners would rebound with a vengeance in 2008. Spearheaded by the outstanding play of sophmore QB Justin Scuorzo, senior 3rd team all-state RB Eric Deery, and an opportunistic defense that posted 4 shutouts and allowed more than 14 points only twice in 12 games, P'burg returned to prominence on the gridiron with an outstanding

10-2 season, finishing as the Star Ledger's #13 ranked team in the state. The season was capped off by claiming another championship, this time the North Jersey Section 2 Group 3 title with a 20-6 win over old rival Rahway. Deery ran for 1,693 yards, the 2nd highest total in P'burg history, and scored 15 TDs, while Scuorzo passed for 1,435 yards in his 1st year as starter. P'burg's undersized defense picked off 21 passes to key the Liners' resurgence. The championship was P'burg's 3rd this decade in 5 tries, and 9th in school history.

Phillipsburg returned another nice core of players in 2009, but questions surrounded the offensive line, which was completely lost to graduation. Coach Bob Stem and his staff were able to put together another efficient unit in the trenches, however, and it paid dividends for the Stateliners. Junior QB Justin Scuorzo once again passed for 1,477 yards, junior RB Dana Lee rushed for 1,109 yards, and the Liners put together another 10-2 season, culminated by another successful run through the state playoffs, this time in Section 2 Group 4, as P'burg routed Ridge 34-7 to claim back-to-back sectional titles for the first time in school history. The sectional title and final ranking at #12 in the Star Ledger capped off the winningest decade in Phillipsburg history, as the Liners chalked up their 88th win, vaulting head coach Bob Stem to within 4 wins of surpassing legendary coach Mike Maloney as the school's winningest coach of all time.

The Stateliners entered the 2010 season with hopes for a 3rd consecutive sectional title with a large nucleus of lettermen returning. The season would prove to be a roller coaster ride of sorts, but would conclude with the program's most satisfying win in years. The Liners torched their first five opponents by a combined 226-41, but ran into a familiar roadblock in mid-season, when 3 lost fumbles inside their own 30 and a last-minute goal line stand by Hunterdon Central would lead to a 28-25 loss to the Red Devils. The Liners rebounded to post two more wins entering the post-season. But P'burg's 42-27 first-round sectional playoff win over Franklin proved to be costly, as 3-year starting QB Justin Scuorzo suffered a concussion. With Scuorzo sidelined with the injury, the Stateliners suffered a heartbreaking last-second 28-21 loss to unbeaten Piscataway, ending their dreams of a 3rd consecutive sectional crown. P'burg entered the Thanksgiving Day clash with once-beaten Easton, who had claimed four consecutive wins over the Liners, determined to claim redemption. With a defensive effort that will go down as one of the finest in series history, P'burg shut down a potent Rover attack to claim a hard-fought 3-0 OT win when senior kicker Anthony Castro booted his school-record 11th FG, sending the Stateliner bench into a frenzy. The 9-2 season proved to be historic in a lot of ways. The Stateliners finished as the 2nd highest scoring team in P'burg history, and set school records for average yards gained per game and per play. Individually, besides Castro's school record FG, Scuorzo became the school's all-time career leader in passing yardage and TD passes, surpassing former Liner star Justin Viscomi. Two-way star Gerald VanDeCruz was named 1st team all-state by the Star Ledger, becoming the 60th Liner to be honored. And the Liners' 9 wins propelled head coach Bob Stem past legendary coach Mike Maloney, making Stem the winningest coach in P'burg history with 112 wins. Just one week after the Thanksgiving Day victory, Stem announced his retirement, bringing his highly successful tenure to a fitting conclusion.

The 2011 season marked the start of a new era, as long-time assistant coach Ryan Ditze succeeded Bob Stem as P'burg head coach. The Stateliners enjoyed a 7-3 season, but once again stumbled versus Hunterdon Central, losing to the Red Devils for the fifth consecutive time, and lost to rival Easton. P'burg also failed to qualify for the sectional playoffs for the first time since 1999.

The 2012 season saw the program take a few steps backward as P'burg suffered a rare losing season, finishing 4-6 and once again failing to qualify for playoffs.

But in 2013, Ditze and the Stateliners got the program back on track. P'burg put together a 10-2 season, losing only to Immaculata 31-28 in 2 OT and to Easton 16-7. The Liners capped off the year by storming through the North 2 Group 4 sectional playoffs, beating Scotch Plains-Fanwood 40-20 and JFK (Iselin) 42-14 before hammering Mendham 39-0 to capture the school's 6th sectional championship. P'burg got outstanding performances from a trio of juniors. RB Joe Maso rushed for 1,565 yards, the 4th highest single season total in P'burg history, and scored 19 TDs, which earned him Star Ledger 1st-team Group 4 honors. He was joined on the Group 4 first team by DB Anthony Guarino, an athletic, versatile performer who excels on offense, defense, and on special teams. In addition, LB Taji Lowe, the team's leading tackler with 79 stops, received 2nd-team Group 4 all-state honors. These outstanding players give the Stateliners a talented core to build their team around for the upcoming 2014 season.

Championships

STATE CHAMPIONSHIPS (11)

(from 1974-1981 and 1995-2013...
*not eligible for state playoffs from 1982-1994)
1918, 1935, 1942, 1949, 1960 1977, 2001, 2005, 2008,
2009, 2013 (state sectional champion)

Phillipsburg Garnet and Grey 1949 NJ State Champions

STATE PLAYOFF APPEARANCES (18)

(from 1974-1981 and 1995-2013...
*not eligible for state playoffs from 1982-1994)
1975, 1977, 1978, 1979, 1981, 1995, 2000, 2001, 2002, 2003, 2004, 2005,
2006, 2007, 2008, 2009, 2010, 2013

STATE CHAMPIONSHIP GAME APPEARANCES (11)

(from 1974-1981 and 1995-2013...
*not eligible for state playoffs from 1982-1994)
1975,1977,1978,1979,2001,2004,2005,2006,2008,2009,2013

CONFERENCE CHAMPIONSHIPS (24)

Big 4: 1935, 1942, 1945*, 1949, 1951#, 1954*, 1955
Big 5: 1960, 1961*, 1963, 1964, 1971*, 1972*
East Penn: 1977*, 1982*, 1983*, 1984, 1990
Skyland: 2000*, 2003, 2004, 2005, 2006
Mid State 38 Delaware Division: 2013
(* indicates co-champion)
(# indicates 4-way tie)

Stateliners celebrate 15-6 win over Piscataway for the 2005 N2
G4 championship, finishing the season 12-0 for the first time in
school history. Photo by Athena and Adam Kita.

NJSIAA STATE PLAYOFF HISTORY

(overall record 26-12 *indicates sectional champion)

***2013 North 2 Group 4: Scotch Plains-Fanwood W 40-20
JFK (Iselin) W 42-14
Mendham W 39-0**

2010 North 2 Group 4: Franklin W 42-27 Piscataway L 28-21

***2009 North 2 Group 4: Piscataway W 19-16 OT Westfield W 35-7
Ridge W 34-7**

***2008 North 2 Group 3: Mendham W 14-0 Irvington W 13-6
Rahway W 20-6**

2007 North 2 Group 4: Franklin L 26-7

2006 North 2 Group 4: North Hunterdon W 41-14 Union W 42-20
Elizabeth L 14-9

***2005 North 2 Group 4: East Orange W 50-20 Union W 56-14
Piscataway W 15-6**

2004 North 2 Group 4: Woodbridge W 34-14 Elizabeth W 14-12
Piscataway L 27-26 OT

2003 North 2 Group 3: Ridge L 31-27

2002 North 2 Group 3: West Morris W 21-3 Jefferson L 27-7

***2001 North 2 Group 4: Plainfield W 21-6 Roxbury W 34-14
Montclair W 10-7**

2000 North 2 Group 4: Montclair L 6-0

1995 North 2 Group 3: Nutley L 21-14

1981 North 2 Group 3: Caldwell L 28-6

1979 North 2 Group 3: Randolph W 22-13 Rahway L 14-6

1978 North 2 Group 3: West Morris W 36-6 Rahway L 23-10

*1977 North 2 Group 3: Rahway W 34-0 Parsippany W 26-0

1975 North 2 Group 3: East Orange W 22-2 Morris Hills L 7-0

Phillipsburg High School
2005 State Champions

UNDEFEATED/TIED SEASONS
1964 8-0-1
1960 8-0-1
1942 9-0-1
1941 7-0-3
1910 5-0-1

1960 North Jersey Section 2 State Champions

OVERALL RECORD
(1905-2013)
650-313-50 (.642 winning pct.)

RECORD AT MALONEY STADIUM
(Oct. 18, 1930-2013)
332-91-15 (.758 winning pct.)

RECORD BY DECADE

1905-1909 21-10-0
1910-1919 49-16-7
1920-1929 30-37-10
1930-1939 53-38-5
1940-1949 72-15-8
1950-1959 63-22-4
1960-1969 58-24-8
1970-1979 60-35-3
1980-1989 74-28-2
1990-1999 52-48-3
2000-2009 88-25-0
2010-2013 30-13-0

STATELINER VICTORY MILESTONES

THE ROAD TO 650

(Games in bold played at Maloney Stadium)

#1 1905 P'burg 20 Allentown 0
#50 1915 P'burg 18 Battin (Elizabeth) 0
#100 1929 P'burg 13 Easton 0
#150 1938 P'burg 7 Bethlehem 0
#200 1946 P'burg 19 Paterson Central 0
#250 1954 P'burg 19 Northampton 0
#300 1961 P'burg 42 William Allen 18
#350 1971 P'burg 12 Bethlehem Freedom 7
#400 1979 P'burg 35 Allentown CC 18
#450 1985 P'burg 48 William Allen 0
#500 1993 P'burg 39 Emmaus 24
#550 2002 P'burg 28 Watchung Hills 25
#600 2007 P'burg 21 Hillsborough 7
#650 2013 P'burg 39 Mendham 0

Liners salute the student body after chalking up victory #600 with a 21-7 win over Hillsborough in 2007.
Photo by Darren Leone.

Honors and Awards

ALL-STATE

(1st team Newark News, Newark Star Ledger, or AP)

1915 Dan Zeigler 1918 Howard Raub 1918 Clayt Willever 1920 Charlie Berry

1928 Ted Dailey 1931 Zolt Stamus 1933 John Carberry 1933 Harold Bellis

1934 Paul Opdyke 1934 Bill VanSyckle 1935 Sammy Moyer 1941 Joe Dilts

1942 Sonny Judson 1942 Earl Reed 1943 Earl Reed 1944 Bill Walsh

1945 Mickey Frinzi 1945 Gene Gallagher 1946 Ray Mantone 1947 Ed Rush

Bill Walsh, an all-state center in 1944, had a distinguished career after graduating from Phillipsburg. After starring at center for four years at Notre Dame, he later earned all-pro honors as a center for the Pittsburgh Steelers. Following his active playing career, Walsh coached in the pros for 32 years with the Dallas Texans, Atlanta Falcons, and the Philadelphia Eagles.

1948 Jim Ringo 1948 Joe Szombathy 1948 Jeep Price 1949 Ron Exley

1949 Russ Dilts 1951 Rich Barbadora 1952 Jim Dalrymple 1953 Ed Allen

1954 George Snyder 1954 Don DeGerolamo 1955 John Tersigni

1957 Bob Stem 1957 Frank Gildner 1958 Marv Lippincott 1958 Greg Matviak

1960 Tom Allen 1960 John Bronico 1961 Jim Dick 1961 Herb Stecker

1963 Charles Stecker 1964 George Hummer 1977 Steve Searfoss

1978 Jim Clymer 1979 Jim Clymer 1981 Mark Klemka 1982 Mark Klemka

1983 Ned Bolcar 1984 Ned Bolcar 1985 Tim Miers 1988 Scott Vaughn

1989 Greg Troxell 1990 Larrame Furman 1995 Mike Lelko 2000 Matt Brunetti

2001 Jason Thomas 2001 Frank Duffy 2003 Brandon Mason

2004 Tim Penyak 2005 Eric Agnew 2010 Gerald VanDeCruz

Stateliner great Bob Stem

TOP TEN PLAYERS of the DECADE
(as chosen by the Star Ledger)

1910-1919 Clayt Willever 1918

1920-1929 Ted Dailey 1927

1930-1939 **Sammy Moyer 1935

1940-1949 Earl Reed 1943
**Russ Dilts 1949

1970-1979 Jim Clymer 1979

1980-1989 *Ned Bolcar 1984

* Ned Bolcar also named one of the Top Ten Defensive Players of the Century

** Sammy Moyer and Russ Dilts were honorable mention

George "Sammy" Moyer

**THE NATIONAL FOOTBALL FOUNDATION
& COLLEGE HALL of FAME**
LEHIGH VALLEY CHAPTER
PHILLIPSBURG INDUCTEES
Jim Ringo 1982
Bill Walsh 1983
Harold Bellis 1985
Joe Szombathy 1995
Les Kish 1996
Mickey Frinzi 1997
Charley Berry 2000
Ned Bolcar 2000
Bob Stem 2004

Jim Ringo

THE NATIONAL FOOTBALL FOUNDATION
& COLLEGE HALL of FAME
LEHIGH VALLEY CHAPTER SCHOLAR ATHLETE

1961 Herb Bagley 1962 Les Kish 1963 Tom Dominic 1964 Wayne Pambianchi 1965 Greg Scott 1966 Jim Bellis 1967 Barry Stacer 1968 Don Jean 1969 Roger Blum 1970 Brian Dominic 1971 Wayne Richline 1972 Mike Kline 1973 Jim Langner 1974 Scott Clark 1975 John Tersigni 1976 RichDewire 1977 Mike Stocker 1978 Mike Ritz 1979 Ron DiBiase 1980 Jim Clymer 1981 Ed Beagell 1982 Mike Echevarria 1983 Ken Green 1984 Chris Troxell 1985 Ned Bolcar 1986 John Sabo 1987 Bill Snyder 1988 Chris LaGulla 1989 Bob Orth 1990 Greg Troxell 1991 Jim Jaroschak 1992 Jarrod Spencer 1993 Glen McNamee 1994 Dan Homa 1995 Joe Luke 1996 Jarrett Hosbach 1997 Justin Curzi 1998 Bob Steele 1999 Justin Bowers 2000 Justin Mannick 2001 Steve Willever 2002 JoeD'Imperio 2003 Kevin Osifchin 2004 Dave Baker 2005 Bob Coyle 2006 Dave Abel 2007 Mark Bigelli 2008 Shane Chalupa 2009 Derek Brousseau 2010 Wolfgang Connell 2011 Nick Porcelli 2012 Rob Waterson 2013 Michael Fitz 2014 Tyler Troxell

1,000 YARD RUNNING BACKS

1977 Mike Ritz 1,111

1989 Larrame Furman 1,274

1990 Larrame Furman 1,415

1994 Joe Luke 1,257

1994 Leonard Moore 1,383

1996 Dave Strahle 1,050

2001 Leonard Brice 1,187

2002 Leonard Brice 1,638

*2003 Brandon Mason 1,880 (*school record)

2004 Justin Gaymon 1,032

2005 Art Wright 1,014

2006 Art Wright 1,258

2008 Eric Deery 1,693

2009 Dana Lee 1,109

2010 Gerald VanDeCruz 1,197

Dana Lee 1,179

2013 Joe Maso 1,565

ALL-TIME LEADING SCORERS

1. Larrame Furman Class of 1991 298 points
2. Art Wright Class of 2007 260 points
3. Leonard Brice Class of 2003 234 points
4. Clayt Willever Class of 1919 195 points
5. Brandon Mason Class of 2004 168 points
6. Joe Luke Class of 1995 158 points
7. Leonard Moore Class of 1995 154 points
8. Eric Deery Class of 2009 150 points
9. Dave Strahle Class of 1997 148 points
10. Dutch Seip Class of 1946 144 points

Art Wright, the 2nd leading scorer in P'burg history, set school records in 2006 for TDs (26) and points scored (158) in a season. Photo by Athena and Adam Kita.

EXPRESS-TIMES PLAYER of the YEAR

1976 Steve McNamee
1984 Ned Bolcar
1990 Larrame Furman
1995 Mike Lelko
2003 Brandon Mason

All-Time Coaching Records

Mike Maloney (1905-1931)...106-77-17 (1918 NJ State Champions)

Art Pursel (1932-1935)...35-3-1 (1935 NJ State Champions)

Whiz Rhinehart (1936-1937)...6-12-1

Doug Krick (1938-1939)...6-11-3

Frank Klein (1940-1951)...84-20-9 (1942 & 1949 NJ State Champions)

Sammy Moyer (1952-1953)...12-5-1

Harold Bellis (1954-1967)...86-29-10 (1960 NJ State Champions)

Mickey Frinzi (1968-1972)...26-18-1

Bob Stem (1973-1981)...56-30-4 (1977 N2 G3 Champions)

Phil Rohm (1982-1986)...38-14

Legendary P'burg coach Frank Klein never played organized football at the high school or collegiate level. Klein attended St. Joseph's parochial school located on the south side of Easton, a school that did not field a football team. He then attended Lafayette College, where he did not participate on the gridiron. Incredibly, Klein's lack of experience on the field was not a hindrance to him as a coach, where he produced an 84-20-9 record including two unbeaten state championship teams in 1942 and 1949. **Note: Klein did participate in service football while serving in the U.S. army at Camp Lee, Virginia.

Phil Rohm

98

Tom Dominic (1987-1989)…25-8

Bruce Smith (1990-1997)…46-34-3

Phil Rohm (2nd term 1998-2004)…47-28 (2001 N2 G4 Champions)

Bob Stem (2nd term 2005-2010)…56-13 (2005 N2 G4,
2008 N2 G3, & 2009 N 2 G4
Champions)

Many football players deal with position changes when moving from high school to the collegiate level. But few players have ever had as unique a change of position as former P'burg coach Harold Bellis. An all-state center in 1933 at Phillipsburg, Bellis proceeded to play QB at Lafayette College. A position change as drastic as this one, which would be unheard of today, reflects on Bellis' versatility as a player as well as a skillful eye for talent on the part of his coach. Obviously, the knowledge of blocking schemes Bellis learned as a lineman and the field generalship he acquired as a quarterback were huge assets during his coaching career, where he fashioned an 86-29-10 record, including two unbeaten teams and a state championship in 1960.

Bob Stem is P'burg's winningest coach of all time with 112 victories.

Ryan Ditze (2011- present)…21-11 (2013 N2 G4 Champions)

School Records

TEAM RECORDS

Most games played in a season: 12 (5x)
Most wins in a season: 12 (2005)
Most points scored in a quarter: 43 vs Newark East Side (1950)
Most Points scored in a game: 101 vs Washington (1918)
Most points scored in a season: 422 (2005)
Most yardage gained in a season: 4,543 yards (2005)
Highest average yards per game: 393 (2010)
Highest average yards per play: 7.69 yards (2010)
Highest average points per game: 48 points (1918)
Consecutive seasons with a 1,000 yard rusher: 6 (2001-2006)
Consecutive wins: 29 (1933-1935)
Fewest points allowed in a season: 6 (1941)

INDIVIDUAL RECORDS

Most points in a game: Clayt Willever 46 vs Lincoln (1919)

Most points in a season: Art Wright 158 in 2006

Most points in a career: Larrame Furman 298

Most PATs in a season: Steve Turner 40 (1989) and Tim Burger (2005)

Most PATs in a career: Steve Turner 67

Most FGs in a season: 9 Alex Toma (2008)

Most FGs in a career: 11 Anthony Castro (2009-2010)

Longest FG: 46 yards Steve Weisel (1986 vs Parkland) and Anthony Castro (2009 vs Scotch Plains)

Phillipsburg once put together a school-record 29-game winning streak. After winning their final eight games in 1933 (all by shutout), they proceeded to go 10-0 in both the 1934 and 1935 seasons. A win in their first game in 1936 was followed by a crushing 50-0 loss to Bloomfield, bringing the streak to an end. Incredibly, P'burg posted shutouts in 25 of the 29 games, outscoring their opponents 510-31 in the most dominant display of football in school history. However, a dark cloud came over the program in the middle of the streak when it was discovered that the garnet and grey had used an ineligible player, QB John Dornish, in the nine games preceding the 1934 Thanksgiving Day clash with Easton. As a result, P'burg was forced to forfeit all nine of those games, and thus, one of the greatest feats in Phillipsburg football history was negated

Most receptions in a game: Mike Lelko 16 (1985)

Most receptions in a season: Mike Lelko 87 (1995) *state record

Most yards gained receiving in a season: Mike Lelko 1,353 (1995) *state record

Most receptions by a RB in a career: Art Wright 61 receptions, 871 yards, 9 TDs

Most interceptions in a game: 3 Wolfgang Connell, Matt Deery, John Stillo, Jim Langner, and Jim Jaroschak

Most interceptions in a season: 10 Jim Jaroschak (1990) and Bob Sharr (1977)

Phillipsburg once scored more than 100 points in a game, beating Washington 101-0 in 1918. P'burg also beat Lincoln of Jersey City 99-0 that same year. For the season, Phillipsburg outscored the opposition 336-13, with all 13 points being scored by Barringer in a 13-6 loss. P'burg finished the season with a 6-1 record and was named New Jersey's first-ever state champion.

Most yards rushing in a game: 305 Brandon Mason (2003) vs Franklin

Most yards rushing in a season: 1,880 Brandon Mason (2003)

Most yards rushing in a career: 3,674 Leonard Brice

Most yards passing in a game: 308 Bill Snyder (1986) vs Freedom

Most yards passing in a season: 1,987 Justin Viscomi (2005)

Most yards passing in a career: 4,232 Justin Scuorzo (2007-2010)

Most TD passes in a game: 5 Justin Viscomi (2005) vs Hillsborough

Most TD passes in a season: 17 Justin Viscomi (2005)

Most TD passes in a career: 37 Justin Scuorzo (2007-2010)

Longest run from scrimmage: 93 yards Nate Johnson (1978) vs Allentown Central Catholic

Longest TD pass: 97 yards Justin Viscomi to Blair Decker (2006) vs Watchung Hills

Longest punt return: 99 yards Zolt Stamus (1933) vs Phillipsburg Parochial

Longest kick return: 100 yards Joe Gebhardt (1915), Tom McDermott (1920), and Ray Koehler (2001)

Longest return of an intercepted pass: 101 yards Josh Merante (1990) vs Bethlehem Liberty

Most blocked punts in a season: 10 Jack Carling (1934)

Most all-purpose yards in a season: 2,300 yards Brandon Mason (2003)

Most varsity games started: 45 Ian Decker (2002-2005)

Most consecutive varsity games started: 45 Ian Decker (2002-2005)

Most TDs in a season: 26 Art Wright (2006)

Most TDs in a career: 49 Larrame Furman

Stateliner Trivia

1. Which team scored the most points ever versus Phillipsburg in a game? How many points did they score? What year?

2. Who was the first running back in P'burg history to rush for more than 1,000 yards in a season? How many yards did he have? What year did he accomplish this feat?

3. Who was Phillipsburg's last opponent at Maloney Stadium prior to its renovation in the 1990s? Who won? What was the score?

4. Which former Phillipsburg player transferred to Easton and later rushed for 190 yards on Thanksgiving Day, helping the Rovers beat the favored Stateliners?

5. In which decade did Phillipsburg have three unbeaten seasons, and four others where they only lost one game?

6. What is the highest scoring game ever played at Maloney Stadium? Who won? What was the score?

7. Which former P'burg player and school record-holder attended junior college in California and then played for the Arizona Wildcats in the PAC 10 conference? What school record does he hold?

8. Name three former P'burg players who won either the MVP award or Outstanding Lineman award versus Easton and four months later won an individual state wrestling championship.

9. What is the fewest number of points ever allowed by Phillipsburg in an entire season? What year did this occur?

10. Name the former Phillipsburg player who ran an interception back for a TD versus Easton when he was only a freshman.

11. In which back-to-back years did Turkey Day fans see an unbeaten P'burg team lose to Easton, followed the next year by an unbeaten Rover team falling to the Stateliners?

12. Which P'burg head coach compiled the highest winning percentage during his tenure at Phillipsburg?

13. In 2003 all-state running back Brandon Mason established the single season rushing record with 1,880 yards. How many times that year did he rush for more than 200 yards in a game, and who were the opponents?

14. What year was the P'burg/Easton game first televised on ESPN? Who won? What was the final score?

15. Which former Stateliner all-state wide receiver set school and state records for receptions and yards receiving in a season during his senior year? How many receptions and yards receiving did he have? Who was the quarterback? What year did he set the records?

16. In 1977, P'burg won its first sectional state title since playoffs had begun in 1974. Who did they defeat in the championship game and what was the score?

17. What was P'burg head coach Bob Stem's record vs P'burg while he was head coach at Bethlehem Catholic in PA?

18. Phillipsburg has had two seasons in which it had two running backs who gained more than 1,000 yards rushing in the same season. What years did this occur and who were the running backs?

19. In 1970, Dave Stetler kicked the winning field goal in the final seconds to defeat Allentown Dieruff. What was the final score?

20. In what year did P'burg begin using the nickname Stateliners?

21. Name the P'burg QB who was named offensive MVP of the P'burg/Easton game when he was only a sophomore. What year did he win the award?

22. Which P'burg player worked with world-renowned oceanographer/deep sea explorer Jacques Cousteau following his graduation from college?

23. In what year did P'burg abandon the single wing and begin using the t-formation?

ANSWERS

(1) Elizabeth, 54, 2012 (2) Mike Ritz, 1,111, 1977 (3) Council Rock (Pa.), P'burg 32-3. (4) Tyrone Randolph (5) 1940s
(6) 1949, P'burg 49 McKinley Tech 35 (7) Nate Johnson, longest run from scrimmage, 93 yards vs ACC in 1978
(8) Buddy Morris, Kevin Kane, Greg Troxell (9) 6, 1941 (10) Malcolm Dock (11) 1954, 1955 (12) Art Pursel 1932-1935 .897%
(13) 4 times: Watchung Hills (207), Franklin (305), Hunterdon Central (300), Ridge (260) (14) 1988, P'burg 20-15
(15) Mike Leiko, 87, 1,353, Keith Kuilman, 1995 (16) Parsippany, 26-0 (17) 9-1
(18) 1994, Joe Luke and Leonard Moore, and 2010 Dana Lee & Gerald VanDeCruz (19) 3-2 (20) 1955 (21) Chris Troxell, 1981
(22) Jim Clymer (23) 1945

About The Author

Dave Leone was born and raised in Phillipsburg, N.J. He is a 1968 graduate of Phillipsburg High School, where he was a 3-sport athlete, earning 7 varsity letters in football, basketball, and track. He was a starting running back on the 1966 and 1967 Phillipsburg football teams, the last two teams guided by legendary coach Harold Bellis. He was a second-team all-East Penn League selection in basketball, setting what was at the time a school record for most points scored in an East Penn League game with 41 versus Tamaqua. His dad Paul Sr. was an all-county guard on P'burg's unbeaten 1942 state championship team, and his late brother Paul Jr. was a third-team all-state selection at guard/nose guard on the 1963 P'burg team that finished 7-1-1. Dave attended Dickinson College and Seton Hall University, and graduated from Moravian College in Bethlehem, Pa. with a B.A. in Management. He is the creator and administrator of statelinerfootball.com, a website dedicated to the history and tradition of Phillipsburg High School football. He retired in December, 2012 after working more than 27 years with the State of New Jersey. He has recently worked for the Easton Express-Times as a freelance sports reporter, with the majority of his articles focused on football and wrestling. Dave has lived all of his life in the Phillipsburg area, and has been a lifelong fan of P'burg athletics, especially football and wrestling.